In the name of Allah,
the Most Gracious, the Most Merciful

Also by
Hedaya Hartford and Ashraf Muneeb

Initiating and Upholding an
Islamic Marriage

Your Islamic Marriage Contract

In Arabic

ذخر المتأهلين والنساء في تعريف الأطهار والدماء (تحقيق)

للإمام محمد بير علي البركوي

منهل الواردين من بحار الفيض على ذخر المتأهلين في مسائل الحيض (تحقيق)

للعلامة ابن عابدين

إرشاد المكلفين إلى دقائق ذخر المتأهلين (تأليف)

Birgivi's Manual Interpreted

Complete Fiqh of Menstruation & Related Issues

Hedaya Hartford • Ashraf Muneeb

First Edition
2006 AC/1427 AH
Reprint
2017 AC /1438 AH

Published by
amana publications
10710 Tucker Street
Beltsville, MD 20705-2223 USA
Tel. 301.595.5777 / 800-660-1777
Fax 301.595.5888, 240.250.3000
Email: amana@amana-corp.com
Website: www.amanapublications.com

1-59008-046-7 (10-digit ISBN) / 978-1-59008-046-7 (13-digit ISBN)

Library of Congress Cataloging-in-Publications Data

Birgivi Mehmet Efendi, ca. 1522-1573.
[Dhukhr al-muta'ahilīn wa-al nisā' fī ma'rīfat al-athār wa-al-dimā'. English & Arabic]
Birgivi's manual interpreted : complete fiqh of menstruation & related issues / Hedaya Hartford, Ashraf Muneeb. -- 1st ed.
p. cm.
ISBN 1-59008-046-7
1. Birgiv[w] Mehmet Efendi, ca. 1522-1573. Dhukhr al-muta'ahilīn wa-al nisā' fī ma'rīfat al-athār wa-al-dimā'. 2. Menstruation--Early works to 1800. 3. Purity, Ritual--Islam--Early works to 1800. 4. Women--Legal status, laws, etc. (Islamic law)--Early works to 1800. 5. Hanafites--Early works to 1800. I. Hartford, Hedaya. II. Muneeb, Ashraf. III. Title.
KBP184.47.M45B573 2006
297.5'7082--dc22

2006030354

Printed by Mega Printing in Turkey

Contents

Part 2: The Commentary in Detail

بسم الله الرحمن الرحيم

الحمد لله الذى قال فى كتابه الكريم : إنما يخشى الله من عباده العلماء والصلاة والسلام على سيدنا ورسولنا محمد الذى جعل العلماء ورثة الأنبياء ، وعلى آله وصحبه الأصفياء .

وبعد :

فيقول العبد الضعيف "محمد أمين سراج" غفر الله له ولوالديه ، ولأبنائه ، ولتلامذته : لما آنست فى الأخ الكريم «أشرف أحمد منيب» ، والأخت الفاضلة «هداية هار تفورد» الاستيعاب والفهم الدقيق لكتاب «ذخر المتأهلين والنساء فى تعريف الأطهار والدماء» للإمام "محمد پير على البركوي» أحد كبار العلماء فى الدولة العثمانية فقد أجزتهما بتدريس هذا الكتاب فى أيّ مكان ، أو بلد نزلا ، بالشروط المعتبرة عند العلماء ، كما أجيزهما بما أجازنى به شيوخى الأفاضل . ومنهم خاتمة العلماء فى الدولة العثمانية ، الشيخ محمد زاهد الكوثري .

هذا ، وإنى أوصيهما ، ونفسى بتقوى الله فى السرّ والعلَن ، واتباع سنة نبيّه الكريم صلى الله عليه وسلّم ، والتعليم لوجه الله تعالى مع الالتزام بعقيدة أهل السنة والجماعة . وأسأل المولى العليّ القدير أن يوفقنى وإياهما لخدمة دينه ، ونشر سنة نبيّه الكريم ، ويغفر لى ، ولهما ، ويحشرنا فى زمرة العلماء الصالحين . والحمد لله ربّ العالمين . فى ٨٠/ رجب الفرد/ ١٤٢٥ هـ

محمد أمين سراج
المدرس فى مسجد السلطان
محمد الفاتح . بإسطنبول
محمد أمين سراج

محمد أمين سراج

الشاهد الأول : عبد الرحمن أرجان البيضوى

الشاهد الثانى : حمدى آرسلان

AUTHORIZATION

In the name of Allah, the Most Gracious, the Most Merciful

Praise to Allah who said in His Majestic Book: 'Only the knowledgeable of His servants fear Allah' (al-Fatir 35:28). And blessings and peace upon our liegelord and Messenger Muhammad, who has made the learned the heirs of the Prophets, and upon his family and his purified Companions.

To commence: The weak slave, Muhammad Amin Siraj, may Allah forgive him, his parents, his children, and his students, says: When I found full comprehension and meticulous understanding of the book *Dhukhr al-Muta'ahhilin wa al-Nisa' fi Ta'rif al-Athar wa al-Dima'* by Imam Muhammad Pir Ali al-Birgivi, one of the great scholars of the Ottoman Empire, in the noble brother Ashraf Ahmed Muneeb and the distinguished sister Hedaya Hartford, I authorized them both to teach this book in any place or country they visit according to the recognized conditions of the scholars, just as I have authorized them both with that which I have been authorized to convey by my distinguished sheikhs, including the seal of the scholars of the Ottoman Empire, Sheikh Muhammad Zahid al-Kawthari.

This, and verily I urge them both and myself to fear Allah secretly and openly; and to follow the sunna of His noble Prophet, may Allah bless him and give him peace; to teach for the sake of Allah Most High with adherence to the tenets of faith of the orthodox Muslims (*Ahl al-Sunna wa al-Jama'a*). And I ask the Lord Most High, Almighty, to grant us success in serving His religion and spreading the sunna of His noble Prophet, may Allah bless him and give him peace, and to forgive us and assemble us on the Day of Judgment among the group of righteous scholars. And all praise is to Allah, Lord of the Worlds.

Composed on 10 Rajab 1425 A.H. [26 August 2004 A.D.]

Muhammad Amin Siraj [signed]
Teacher at the Sultan Muhammad al-Fatih Mosque in Istanbul

First witness: Abdul Rahman Arjan al-Bensawi [signed]

Second witness: Hamdi Arsalan [signed]

In the name of Allah,
the Most Gracious, the Most Merciful

INTRODUCTION

Praise be to Allah, Lord of the Worlds, who shows whomever He wills the path to eternal happiness, the sunna of His beloved Prophet (Allah bless him and give him peace).

In 2005 we published in Arabic an edited and annotated version of Imam Birgivi's treatise *Dhukhr al-Muta'ahhilin wa al-Nisa' fi Ta'rif al-Athar wa al-Dima'* and Imam Ibn 'Abidin's commentary of it, *Manhal al-Waridin min Bihar al-Fayd 'ala Dhukhr al-Muta'ahhilin fi Masa'il al-Hayd*, along with our own commentary *Irshad al-Mukallafin ila Daqa'iq Dhukhr al-Muta'ahhilin*. Alhamdulillah, now we have the opportunity to present this material in English.

The first part of this book, 'The Primary Text,' contains an explanative translation and partial rearrangement of the treatise by Imam Birgivi, may Allah be well pleased with him, along with essential clarifications taken from Imam Ibn 'Abidin's commentary *Manhal al-Waridin*. In addition, other relevant texts as well as our own remarks have been added to clarify or simplify difficult points; these supplementary notations are parenthesized. The texts contain the full citation including the author's name, title, volume, and page number. Our remarks are introduced with a lowercase *t*. The second part of this book, 'The Commentary in Detail,' further elaborates and simplifies the rulings and applications found in the treatise.

We chose this text because of its resourcefulness, precision and reliability. For those interested in Birgivi's treatise, we have included the Arabic text in Appendix 1. According to Imam Ibn 'Abidin this treatise by Imam Birgivi is the principal reference for menstruation, lochia and their related rulings in the Hanafi school of fiqh (jurisprudence). In his commentary *Manhal al-Waridin* he describes the treatise by saying:

> I found it, in spite of its brevity and elegance of verse, comprehensive of the prime sections of this chapter [of menstruation], stripped of elongation and long-windedness, a work of genius unmatched, and no eye has seen aught that rivals it.

For this reason, we have confined ourselves to its presentation of the soundest positions and have reiterated them in the 'Comprehensive Precepts' (*al-qawaid al-kulliya*). We have omitted the section on the woman who has forgotten her habit (def: 3.35), as this problem is usually fixed with medication in our time. If it is not, a scholar with specialized knowledge of menstruation must be consulted. A few points parenthesized in the Arabic text have also been omitted.

We would like to note that finding the exact equivalent in English to some of the specialized terminology of fiqh is difficult. Therefore, throughout this book, we have used the Arabic terms rather than the English definitions of the following: *istihada* (dysfunctional uterine/vaginal bleeding), *tuhr* (the state free of menses or lochia), and *kursuf* (cotton or the like which is placed between the labia minora at the opening orifice of the vagina). *Tuhr* can also mean normal vaginal discharge, but we have used the English term in this case. 'Legal' in this text means 'according to Sacred Law rulings.'

Imam Birgivi mentions seventeen different case studies: five lochial cases and twelve menstrual cases. In the 'Lochial Case Studies' and 'Menstrual Case Studies' sections, we have clearly illustrated each situation and have given a detailed analysis of each case. We have included four additional cases to exemplify other situations. These case studies assimilate the knowledge of lochia and menstruation to show how it is applied in actual situations.

We conclude the book with a simplified medical section because of the overall lack of knowledge in this area. Its purpose is to give a general overview and not to diagnose problems. If a woman is having gynecological problems, she should consult a health practitioner.

The Importance of This Topic

Menstruation is among the most difficult topics in the study of fiqh. The significance of this knowledge is apparent by the detriment caused by the ignorance of it. Attentiveness to these rulings is vital because of the consequences they have on rulings of purification, prayer, reading the Qur'an, fasting, spiritual retreat, pilgrimage, reaching puberty, marital relations, divorce, the waiting period after divorce, and others. Muslims must become familiar with these rulings; otherwise, they will commit forbidden (*haram*) acts without even realizing it. In the introduction of the treatise Imam Birgivi says:

> The jurists have agreed on the obligatoriness of the 'personally obligatory religious knowledge' (*'ilm al-hal*) for all those women and men who believe in Allah and the Day of Judgment. Consequently, the knowledge of the different types of blood pertinent to women is obligatory for women, husbands, and guardians. However, in our time, this was forsaken, or worse–it became as though it were nothing. They [the people of the author's time] do not separate between menstruation, lochia, and istihada, and they do not differentiate between the valid and invalid types of blood and tuhr.

He goes on to explain how he spent a good portion of his life regulating the rulings of menstruation and lochia such that he differentiated between the correct, incorrect, weak, and strong opinions, as well as giving precedence to the soundest positions in the Hanafi school (*madhhab*). He cautions hasty criticism of his deductions because they differ from ones the reader might be familiar with, given the enormity of making a mistake in religious matters.

The Intent of This Book

The intent of this book is to facilitate an understanding of the legal rulings of menstruation and lochia as they pertain to many aspects of our daily lives. The minimal objective is to give readers the ability to recognize a problem but not necessarily solve it, and to realize when they must consult a specialist.

This book, if Allah wills, will answer a wide variety of common questions, while providing a general understanding of the fiqh (jurisprudence) of menstruation and lochia. There is much repetition because we have found through our teaching experience that repetition is instrumental in becoming familiar with the fiqh details and concepts of this subject.

It is important to understand that reading this book does not qualify readers to teach this science until they have studied it with a specialist. Students studying alone often assume they have mastered a subject when in reality this is not the case. It is only when students can confirm their understanding under a teacher that they are assumed to have command of the subject.

How to Read This Book

It is recommended that you read the book from beginning to end in order to grasp the technical vocabulary and consequential rulings, especially for those unfamil-iar with the fiqh of menstruation and lochia.

As the scholars have mentioned, this subject is difficult. Since fiqh texts in general tend to be very dense, a reader unfamiliar with fiqh may either feel overwhelmed by the details or, quite the opposite, believe the details to be insignificant. This can make utilizing the knowledge very difficult.

The reader should anticipate having to read the book a few times and should endeavor not to become frustrated or discouraged. It takes effort and patience to become familiar with the rulings until one can understand them fully, and then apply them.

Several changes have been made to the format of the Arabic text when translating into English. Paragraphs of the text have been numbered to facilitate cross-reference, and titles and subtitles have been added. The abbreviation (def:) is used to mean 'defined at another ruling', and (dis:) is used to mean 'discussed at another ruling.'

Columns of examples or instances of a ruling's applicability are itemized by numbers: 1., 2., 3., and so on, indicating that not all need exist, but any one of them suffices to apply the ruling, such as reaching puberty, the existence of any of which establishes it.

Columns of required conditions or integrals, meaning that all of them must be present for the ruling to hold true, are itemized by letters: a), b), c), and so on. An example is the conditions for the validity of the excused (*ma'dhur*) status, which must all be met for ablution to be valid.

May Allah Most High bless all who read this book with success in following His beloved Messenger (Allah bless him and give him peace) in all acts of worship and practice. And may Allah Most Generous bless us with an increase of *baraka,* understanding, and the love of Allah and His Messenger (Allah bless him and give him peace) in this world and the next. Ameen.

Thursday, Sha'ban 15, 1427
September 7, 2006
Amman, Jordan

Authors' Preface

In the name of Allah, the Most Merciful, the Most Compassionate. Praise to Allah, Lord of the Worlds. Praise to Him who guides us to Islam. And blessings and peace upon our beloved Prophet Muhammad, the exemplar of the righteous, and upon his family and Companions one and all, those who followed after them, and all the righteous.

Only through the blessings and grace of Allah Most High is success given; and even though we have done our best, all mistakes are ours. May Allah protect us and take us by our hand. We ask Allah, Mighty and Majestic, to make this work purely for His sake. We give many thanks to and ask Allah Most Generous to greatly bless Sheikh Hassan al-Hindi of Damascus who acquainted us with this thesis of Imam Birgivi, as well as spent many hours teaching us and answering our questions; and to reward out of His generosity all those who have taught us, those who have helped in editing and making this work, and those who read it. May Allah reward them all abundantly in this world and the next, and accept this humble offering on our behalf. Ameen.

If the reader finds any mistakes, please inform us so they can be corrected for future editions. You can contact us at:

amedits@gmail.com

or

P O Box 961329
Sports City, 11196
Amman, Jordan

Part 1

The Primary Text

قَال النَّبي ﷺ: « مَنْ يُرِدِ اللهُ بِهِ خَيْراً يُفَقِّهْهُ فِي الدِّينِ »

The Prophet (Allah bless him and give him peace) said:

Whoever Allah wants good for
He gives sound understanding of the religion

1

Sacred Law Rulings

There are twelve overall rulings particular to menstruation and lochia: eight are shared between them; and four are specific to menstruation.

During Menstruation or Lochia

1.1 (*t*: In regards to worship, fard is the obligatory, wajib is the necessary, sunna is the recommended, and nafl is the optional.)

1.2 (*t*: Most of the following rulings relate to unlawful (haram) acts. Leaving them because they are unlawful is in itself an act of worship.

A woman need not feel deprived of certain types of worship during these states because she is actually worshipping Allah Most High the way He wishes by her obedience to His command.

She should not consider this time a 'vacation' from worshipping Allah because He has not created us except to worship Him. Therefore, it is recommended during these times that she make dhikr (remembrance of Allah).)

Prayer

1.3 It is unlawful to perform the ritual prayer (whether it is fard, wajib, sunna, or nafl).

1.4 One does not make up prayers missed because of menses or lochia.

1.5 It is recommended that at each prayer time a woman make ablution with the intention of 'drawing near to Allah,' and go to the place in her home where she normally prays. She should sit there and make dhikr (e.g. 'Subhana Llah' and 'Al-hamdu li Llah') for the amount of time she would usually spend in prayer. (Ibn 'Abidin has narrated that if she does this, the reward of her best prayer ever prayed will be written for her (*Hashiya* 2.266).)

1.6 It is unlawful to make the prostration of Qur'an recital if a woman hears a Qur'anic verse (ayah) of prostration, nor is she obliged to make it up later.

1.7 It is unlawful to make the prostration of thankfulness.

1.8 (Ibn 'Abidin: If a woman hears the adhan (the call to prayer), she is not required to repeat it because she is not required to pray at this time (*Hashiya* 2.620).)

(*t*: Instead, she can invoke blessings on the Prophet (may Allah bless him and give him peace) or make any other type of dhikr, such as 'Subhana Llahi wa l-hamdu li Llahi wa la ilaha illa Llahu wa Llahu Akbar'.)

1.9 If menses start while a woman is praying a sunna or nafl prayer, she is obliged to make up that prayer after her menstruation ends.

1.10 If a woman is praying a vowed (nadhr) prayer and her menses start, she is obliged to make it up.

1.11 If a woman is praying an obligatory prayer and her menses start, she is not obliged to make it up after her menstruation ends.

1.12 If a woman makes a vow 'to pray during her menses', she is not obliged to fulfill it because it is unlawful to pray at this time.

1.13 Whether or not a woman is qualified for prayer is determined at the end of each prayer time (dis: 6.11-16, 6.38-39).

FASTING

1.14 It is unlawful to fast. (*t*: If a woman does not eat all day she is sinning, and this is not considered fasting because being free of menses or lochia is one of the stipulations of fasting.)

1.15 One is required to make up all missed fasts.

1.16 If a woman sees blood just minutes before the sun sets, then her fast (whether it is obligatory, wajib, sunna or nafl) is vitiated and she must make it up.

1.17 If a woman makes a vow 'to fast during her menses', she is not obliged to fulfill it because it is unlawful to fast during menstruation.

1.18 (al-Shurunbulali:) If menses or lochia start during the day in Ramadan, it is necessary to eat or drink; it is unlawful for her to imitate those fasting in Ramadan (*Imdad al-Fatah* 660).

(*t*: Eating, however, should be done discreetly and not in public.)

1.19 (*t*: It is unlawful for women to organize a gathering of menstruating women to eat during a day in Ramadan because of the sacredness of the month. However, if two menstruating women happen to meet and eat, then this is permissible.)

READING THE QUR'AN

1.20 It is unlawful to read the Qur'an, even less than a complete ayah (verse), with the intention that it is Qur'an.

If one rinses out one's mouth, this does not remove the prohibition.

(*t*: Reading means to say aloud or to move one's lips; however, just reading with one's eyes and/or saying the words in one's heart silently is not considered reading, and it is permissible.)

1.21 If a woman reads Qur'anic ayahs that are used for dua (supplication) or praise, and her intention is dua or praise, it is permissible.

For example, if she reads the Fatiha (the opening surah (chapter) of the Qur'an) with the intention of praise and/or dua, then during this time she may continue to read it with the same intention.

1.22 It is permissible to use everyday expressions that are partial Qur'anic ayahs such as 'bismi Llah' (in the name of Allah) to begin something, or 'al-hamdu li Llah' (praise be to Allah) to give thanks to Allah, or 'la hawla wa la quwwata illa bi Llah' (there is no power nor strength save through Allah) in times of trouble.

1.23 It is permissible for a Qur'an teacher to read the ayah word by word, such that she stops after each word.

1.24 It is disliked to read the Bible, Torah, or the Book of Psalms, as they are revelations, except for the parts that have been changed.

1.25 It is not disliked to read or say any duas such as the *Qunut* dua, as well as any other type of remembrance of Allah (dhikr).

1.26 It is permissible to look at the Qur'an.

TOUCHING THE QUR'AN

1.27 It is unlawful to touch the Qur'an or a Qur'anic verse (ayah).

1.28 It is unlawful to touch a coin or sheet of paper (lauh) that has a complete Qur'anic ayah written on it (*t*: if there is nothing else written on it).

1.29 It is unlawful to touch the cover of the Qur'an if it is permanently attached to it.

1.30 It is permissible to touch the cover if it is completely removable from the Qur'an, but not the actual Qur'an.

1.31 It is permissible to pick up the Qur'an with a separate barrier (*t*: e.g. a piece of cloth), but not with a part of one's clothing while wearing it.

1.32 If Qur'anic ayahs (verses) are included in any book, such as a book of jurisprudence, it is permissible to touch the book and the pages but not the actual ayahs.

1.33 It is permissible but disliked to touch books of duas and dhikrs.

1.34 It is unlawful to touch jewelry, plates, cups, and so forth that have written on them any Qur'an.

1.35 It is unlawful to wear a necklace, bracelet, or such that has a Qur'anic surah (chapter) or ayah written upon it during the state of:

1. minor ritual impurity;
2. or major ritual impurity;
3. or menses;
4. or lochia;

because of it touching one's body or one's clothing.

1.36 If a Qur'anic surah or ayah is worn as an amulet (ta'weedh), then it should be properly covered and wrapped.

1.37 A translation and/or commentary (tafsir) of the Qur'an has the same rulings as the Qur'an.

1.38 It is unlawful to write the Qur'an or an ayah unless done while not actually touching the paper or whatever she is writing it on. (*t*: She may place a tissue or another piece of paper under her hand, such that her hand does not touch the paper upon which the Qur'an is written.)

ENTERING A MOSQUE

1.39 It is unlawful to enter a mosque except in the case of an emergency, such as the fear of an animal attacking, extreme cold, or extreme thirst. In this case, it is recommended that she first make dry ablution (tayammum) before entering the mosque.

1.40 If a woman is doing a spiritual retreat (i'tikaf) and her menses start, she must leave the mosque immediately and the retreat is vitiated.

1.41 It is permissible to enter the places of Eid prayer if it is held out in the open, but not if held in a mosque.

1.42 It is permissible for her to visit a graveyard.

CIRCUMAMBULATING THE KA'ABA

1.43 It is unlawful to circumambulate the Ka'aba (tawaf).

1.44 If a woman performs an obligatory circumambulation of the Ka'aba during menstruation or lochia, the obligatory circumambulation is valid but she must slaughter a camel to remove the sin of doing so in either of these states.

(*t*: Many scholars say if she is tied to a group or travel arrangement, she may make the obligatory circumambulation and then slaughter a camel in order to be released from *ihram* (the state of consecration that pilgrims enter for hajj or 'umra).)

1.45 (*t*: If menstruation starts while circumambulating the Ka'aba, one leaves the masjid immediately.)

1.46 (Ibn 'Abidin:) If a woman performs a non-obligatory circumambulation in either of these states, then she must slaughter a sheep.

1.47 If one performs an obligatory circumambulation without ablution, then one must slaughter a sheep.

1.48 If one performs a wajib circumambulation without ablution, then one must give charity.

1.49 All the above slaughtering or charity must take place in the Meccan Sacred Precinct (Haram).

1.50 If one repeats the circumambulation in a state of ritual purity before leaving Mecca, then one need not slaughter.

(*Hashiya* 7.259, 7.263)

INTIMATE CONTACT

1.51 Sexual intercourse is unlawful.

1.52 It is unlawful for the husband to touch the skin between the navel and the knees of his wife.

1.53 It is permissible to enjoy one's wife in any other legal way.

1.54 If sexual intercourse occurs, it is a major sin that requires repentance.

1.55 It is recommended, in the event of sexual intercourse, that:

1. If the blood was red, then 4.25 grams of gold (or its equivalence in money) be given in charity.
2. If the blood was yellow, then 2.125 grams of gold (or its equivalence in money) be given in charity.

RITUAL PURITY

1.56 Taking a purificatory bath (ghusl, def: 2.21) is obligatory as soon as the bleeding ends.

1.57 If a woman cannot use water, then she is obliged to make tayammum (dry ablution).

SPECIFIC TO MENSTRUATION

The following four rulings are decisively determined by menstruation:

PUBERTY

1.58 Menstruation establishes puberty.

1.59 (*t*: This makes the female religiously obliged to fulfill all her religious duties as she is legally no longer considered a child, even if only 9 lunar years old (8 solar years and 8 months and 3 weeks).)

1.60 (al-Abyani:) A pubescent male or female may not be married without their permission.

1.61 Puberty is established for a female after the age of 9 lunar years by:

1. her first menstrual period;
2. or becoming pregnant;

3. or having a wet dream;
4. or reaching the age of 15 lunar years (14 solar years, 6 months, and 2 weeks).

1.62 For a male, puberty is established after the age of 12 lunar years (11 solar years, 7 months, and 2 weeks) by:

1. having a wet dream;
2. or causing a pregnancy;
3. or reaching the age of 15 lunar years.

(*Sharh al-Ahkam* 1.57, 2.225-226)

SUNNA OR BIDA' DIVORCE

1.63 The menstrual period distinguishes between the sunna divorce and the innovated (bida') divorce.

1.64 To divorce one's wife during menstruation is unlawful (haram), but in spite of this the divorce is valid. This type of divorce is called an innovated (bida') divorce.

1.65 (Ibn 'Abidin:) The sunna way to divorce one's wife is to do so during a tuhr where there has been no sexual contact.

1.66 If a woman asks for a divorce or a divorce for payment (khula'), or she has the right to divorce herself and does so, then it is permissible even if during her menses.

(*Hashiya* 9.113).

POSTMARITAL WAITING PERIOD ('IDDA)

1.67 Menstruation confirms the end of the waiting period ('idda) after a divorce or khula'. (*t*: The postmarital waiting period ends with the completion of the third menstrual period after the divorce or khula'.)

1.68 (Ibn 'Abidin:) A divorce given during menstruation is a valid divorce even though doing so is prohibited. In this case, the menstrual period she is in does not count towards fulfilling her waiting period.

(*t*: For example, a woman has a 5-day menstrual habit and a 20-day tuhr habit. Her husband divorces her on day 4 of her menses.

a) The divorce is valid and her waiting period starts immediately, but the present menstrual period does not count as the first menstrual period.

b) She must finish her menses (i.e. day 4 and day 5) and tuhr of 20 days, and then the start of the next menses is considered the first of the three menstrual periods that complete the postmarital waiting period.

In this case, she will have a 77-day waiting period:

2 + 20 + (5 + 20 + 5 + 20 + 5).)

1.69 It is sunna to take the wife back after divorcing her during her menstrual period. One should then wait for her to finish her menses, a tuhr, and then another menstrual period. In the tuhr following the second menstrual period in which there has been no sexual contact, the husband may divorce his wife if he is determined; and this would constitute another divorce.

1.70 If a husband divorces his pregnant wife, her waiting period ends as soon as she gives birth. It does not matter if the waiting period is a few hours or months.

(*Hashiya* 9.107-113).

ATONEMENT (KAFFARA)

1.71 Menstruation does not vitiate the consecutiveness of fasting the 60-day atonement.

1.72 (Ibn 'Abidin:) Lochia vitiates the continuity of the 60-day atonement fast.

1.73 Ramadan and both Eids vitiate the consecutiveness in fasting for any type of atonement.

1.74 Bleeding that transforms into istihada (def: 3.14 (5-7)) vitiates the continuity of the 60-day atonement fast.

(*Hashiya* 10.174)

RULINGS FOR THE STATE OF MAJOR RITUAL IMPURITY (JANABA)

1.75 The rulings are the same as the 'eight' shared between lochia and menses (above, 1.3-57), except that one in the state of major ritual impurity (janaba):

1. is obliged to perform the prayer (*t*: must take a bath (ghusl) and perform the prayer on time);
2. is permitted to fast (*t*: the fast is valid even if one takes a bath (ghusl) after sunrise);

3. is permitted to have sexual intercourse, even if before making ablution (*t*: which is sunna to do in this case);
4. is recommended to wash one's hands and rinse one's mouth before eating or drinking.

1.76 It is permissible to leave one's house for a need before taking a bath (ghusl) or making ablution.

1.77 (al-Tahtawi:) It is disliked to trim one's nails and remove bodily hair (*t*: because this state can easily be removed by taking a bath (ghusl).) (*Hashiya al-Tahtawi* 430).

RULINGS FOR THE STATE OF MINOR RITUAL IMPURITY (HADATH)

1.78 It is unlawful to pray or make any type of prostration that is obligatory or otherwise.

1.79 It is unlawful to touch anything that has a complete Qur'anic ayah (verse) written on it.

1.80 It is unlawful to touch a book of Qur'anic commentary (tafsir), even if one washes one's hand.

1.81 It is permissible for an adult with ablution to pass the Qur'an to a prepubescent child, without ablution, who is learning the Qur'an.

1.82 It is permissible to touch books of Hadith, fiqh, and dhikrs; however, it is preferred that one does not.

1.83 It is permissible to recite the Qur'an.

1.84 It is permissible to enter the mosque; but it is disliked because of not being able to pray the 'greeting of the mosque' (tahiyat al-masjid) prayer.

1.85 It is disliked to circumambulate the Ka'aba (dis: 1.44-50).

SUPPLEMENTARY RULINGS

(*t*: We have gathered the following rulings to complement this chapter.)

TRIMMING THE NAILS

1.86 It is permissible to trim one's nails during menstruation or lochia (dis: 1.77).

(*t:* People often confuse the rulings of menses, lochia and major ritual impurity because many hadiths mention them together; however, as mentioned above, not all of their rulings are shared (dis: 1.75).)

REMOVING BODILY HAIR

1.87 It is permissible to remove bodily hair during menstruation or lochia (dis: 1.77).

DIVORCE

1.88 (Ibn 'Abidin:) Divorcing one's wife during her menstruation or lochia is unlawful (haram).

1.89 If a husband does so, the divorce is valid but he is sinful.

1.90 Conversely, it is permissible for a woman to divorce herself during this time if she has the right to do so, or for her to ask for khula' (a divorce for payment).

(*Hashiya* 9.109, 113).

WAITING PERIOD AFTER DIVORCE

1.91 (al-Abyani:) The waiting period after divorce ('idda) is completed by one of the following:

1. If a woman has ever had a menstrual period and is between the ages of 9 and 55, then her waiting period is over at the end of her third menstrual period.
2. If a woman is pregnant, then her waiting period ends with childbirth, regardless of the length of the waiting period.

   For example, if a husband divorces his wife while she is in labor:

   a) her waiting period ends as soon as she gives birth.
   b) If she is pregnant with twins, then it ends after the second child is delivered.
3. If she is someone who has never had a menstrual period, or is younger than 9 or older than 55 and no longer menstruates, her waiting period ends after three full months from the time of the divorce.

1.92 A woman in her postmarital waiting period for either a revocable or finalized divorce must remain at home.

1.93 The husband must provide his divorced wife during her postmarital waiting period with food, drink, clothes, and housing.

1.94 When her postmarital waiting period ends, she vacates the marital house if it is not owned by her.

1.95 During the waiting period, the divorced wife may only leave the house out of extreme necessity, such as needing medical attention, fear that the house may collapse, harassment from household members, and so forth.

WAITING PERIOD AFTER DEATH OF HUSBAND

1.96 The waiting period for a widow is 4 months and 10 days.

1.97 If a woman is pregnant, it ends at childbirth.

1.98 She may leave home during the day to fulfill her needs, such as work, if she has no means of support, or medical attention; she must spend the night at home.

1.99 During the waiting period, a woman should avoid adornment and dressing up or explicitly speaking about marriage, such as getting engaged or its prelude until the waiting period is over.

(*Sharh al-Ahkam* 1.429-448)

2

TERMINOLOGY

These terms are defined in accordance to their legal rulings and usage in the Sacred Law.

2.1 **Blood or Bleeding** (dam): all colored discharge that is not white.

2.2 **Menses** (hayd): blood that exits from the uterus through the vagina of a female at least 9 lunar years old (8 solar years and 8 months and 3 weeks). Menses is not the blood after giving birth, during pregnancy, or caused by illness.

2.3 **Lochia** (nifas): postnatal bleeding that exits from the uterus through the vagina following the delivery of most of the baby. 'Most' means if head first, then after the chest comes out. If feet first, then after the naval comes out. A lochia cannot be preceded by another lochia without a minimal tuhr interval of 6 months in between.

2.4 **Istihada** (dysfunctional uterine/vaginal bleeding): any vaginal bleeding that is not menstruation or lochia. It is invalid blood or invalid bleeding.

2.5 **Valid blood** (dam sahih): for menstruation, bleeding that is minimally 3 days (72 hours) and does not exceed 10 days (240 hours). For lochia, bleeding that does not exceed 40 days (960 hours).

2.6 **Legal blood** (dam hukmi): an interval that the Sacred Law considers to be blood when there is no actual blood.

2.7 **Possible days of menstruation**: from day 1 through day 10, i.e. starting with the first show of blood to the completion of the 240 hours.

2.8 **Possible days of lochia**: from day 1 through day 40, i.e. from the birth of most of the child to the completion of the 960 hours.

2.9 **Tuhr**: the state free of menses or lochia.

2.10 **Valid tuhr** (tuhr sahih): a tuhr of at least 15 days (360 hours) that is not mixed with blood and is between two valid bloods.

2.11 **Legal tuhr** (tuhr hukmi): vaginal bleeding that the Sacred Law regards as tuhr.

2.12 **Invalid tuhr** (tuhr fasid): tuhr less than 15 days or mixed with blood.

2.13 **Mixed tuhr** (tuhr mutakhallil): a tuhr interval between two bloods within the possible days of lochia. A mixed tuhr is a type of invalid tuhr.

2.14 **Complete tuhr** (tuhr tam): a tuhr that is 15 days (360 hours) or more.

2.15 **Incomplete tuhr** (tuhr naqis): a tuhr less than 15 days (360hours).

2.16 **Habit** ('ada): there is a menstrual habit, a tuhr habit, and a lochial habit. Habit refers to the most recent valid blood and tuhr, or the last valid blood, or the last valid tuhr.

2.17 **Beginner** (mubtadi'a): menarche or menstrual beginner refers to the one who is having her first menstrual period. Lochial beginner refers to the one who is having her first lochia.

2.18 **A woman with a habit** (mu'taada): for menstruation this refers to a woman with a previous valid menstrual period and tuhr or a valid menstrual period or a valid tuhr. For lochia this refers to a woman that has a previous lochia.

2.19 **A lost** (mudalla) or **confused** (muhayyara) **woman**: a woman with constant bleeding who has forgotten her menstrual and/or lochial habit.

2.20 **Kursuf**: cotton or the like which is placed between the labia minora (literally, small lips) *at* the opening orifice of the vagina, not *in* the opening.

2.21 **Purificatory bath** (ghusl): (Ibn 'Abidin:) the obligatory integrals of ghusl are to rinse the mouth, nose, and entire body; the external orifice of the genitals, and skin underneath the eyebrows; and to wet thoroughly the navel and inside any hole which is not sealed (e.g. earring hole) (*Hashiya* 1.504-6).

Included in the ghusl time is the time to prepare for it (i.e. to get the water, warm it, and get undressed) and the time after it (i.e. to get dressed).

2.22 **Preferred prayer time**: (Ibn 'Abidin:) for women it is in regard to the 'Asr (midafternoon) prayer time; it is from the start of the prayer time up until the sun goes pale which is about 20 minutes before sunset. Note: there are additional 'preferred prayer times' specific to men in regard to praying in a group at the mosque (*Hashiya* 2.509-520).

2.23 **Place** (makan) or **Time** (zaman): the expected occurrence of menses or tuhr in the habitual cycle.

2.24 **Number** ('adad): the number of days or the duration of menses, lochia or tuhr according to the habit or the changing of the habit.

3

The Basics

3.1 (*t:* When there is a conflict between the Sacred Law and medical analysis of a situation, the Sacred Law takes precedence.

For example, it is medically possible for a woman to menstruate after 12 days of tuhr, but according to the Sacred Law this blood is istihada (dysfunctional bleeding).)

3.2 (*t:* General rulings are made to cover common situations, and any situation that is unusual needs to be discussed with a specialist of menstruation.)

3.3 (*t:* In books of fiqh (jurisprudence) all Sacred Law references to years or age are based on the lunar and not the solar calendar.)

3.4 There are three types of vaginal bleeding pertinent to women: menstruation, lochia, and istihada.

3.5 The menstrual or lochial period ends with either normal white or clear vaginal discharge (tuhr), or with the absence of any discharge at all.

Valid Blood

3.6 The minimal menstrual period is 3 complete days (72 hours).

3.7 There is no stipulation that bleeding be continuous; rather, it is possible that bleeding be intermittent.

The following two cases are examples of a valid menstrual period:

1. One has a spot of blood on Sunday morning at 7:00 A.M. and does not see anything again until Wednesday morning at 6:45 A.M., at which time the bleeding continues until 7:05 A.M.

2. One sees a constant flow from Sunday morning at 7:00 A.M. to Wednesday morning at 7:00 A.M.

Each case is considered a menstrual period.

In either case, if the bleeding ceases just before 7:00 A.M. on Wednesday and one does not see blood for the next 15 days, the blood is not considered menses, rather it is istihada since it is less than 72 hours.

3.8 The maximum menstrual period is 10 complete days (240 hours).

3.9 There is no minimal duration for lochia.

3.10 If a woman gives birth and the bleeding ceases immediately afterwards, then she must take a purificatory bath (ghusl, def:2.21) and pray.

3.11 The maximum lochial period is 40 complete days (960 hours).

3.12 A valid blood cannot be succeeded by a valid blood, such as:

1. two menstrual periods;
2. or two lochial periods;
3. or a lochial and a menstrual period.

There must be a complete tuhr that separates each valid blood.

3.13 Bleeding caused by medication during the possible days of menstruation is menstruation.

INVALID BLOOD

3.14 Types of istihada (dysfunctional bleeding) are:

1. bleeding from a female under the age of 9 lunar years;
2. colored discharge, other than red, from a menopausal woman over 55 lunar years old (53 solar years and 4 months) that is unlike her pre-menopausal menses;
3. bleeding during pregnancy;
4. bleeding that exceeds the maximum for menses or lochia;
5. bleeding less than the minimum during the possible days of menstruation;
6. bleeding in the possible days of menstruation that exceeds the habit and goes over the maximum;

7. bleeding that exceeds the habit and maximum and does not appear in its habitual place:

   (*t*: For example, a woman has a 5-day menstrual habit and a 25-day tuhr habit:

   1. She sees one day of blood before her habitual place and nothing in her habitual place and then sees 7 days of blood.
   2. Here the 1 day plus the 5 habitual days (even though there is no blood) plus 7 days exceed the maximum.
   3. She returns to her habit. Even though there is no actual blood during her 5 habitual days, it is considered legal blood.
   4. The blood before and after her habitual days are istihada);

8. bleeding during the possible days of lochia that exceeds the habit and exceeds the maximum.

3.15 Istihada blood is impure (najis). (Ibn 'Abidin:)

1. It nullifies ablution (dis: 9.1-38).
2. It does not necessitate a bath (ghusl).
3. Praying and fasting are obligatory.
4. Sexual intercourse is permissible.

(*Hashiya* 2.291-2).

3.16 The duration of legal tuhr and any tuhr that has invalid blood is also labeled istihada.

TUHR

3.17 A complete tuhr (the state free of menses or lochia) must separate:

1. two menstrual periods;
2. or two lochias;
3. or a lochia and a menstrual period.

3.18 The minimal tuhr interval between two menstrual periods or a lochia and menstrual period is 15 complete days (360 hours).

3.19 The minimal tuhr interval between two lochias is 6 months (180 days); or 177 days if the previous lochia ended on the first day of the lunar month.

3.20 An incomplete tuhr interval between two bloods does not separate between them. It takes the ruling of legal blood (dis:11.10).

3.21 The mixed tuhr during the possible days of lochia takes the ruling of legal blood, even if the tuhr is 15 days or more.

For example, after giving birth a woman has 5 days of blood, 15 days of tuhr, 5 days of blood, then 15 days of tuhr, and then constant blood.

The first 25 days are lochia because the first 15 days of tuhr is a mixed tuhr and joins the blood before and after it.

3.22 Legal tuhr requires that all obligatory acts of worship be performed.

(*t*: This means that even though one has istihada, according to the Sacred Law one is in legal tuhr, and as such one must pray, fast and may have sexual intercourse.)

3.23 There is no maximum tuhr. It could last a lifetime.

3.24 A tuhr maximum is set at 2 months when there is a need for it during a postmarital waiting period. (*t*: 'Need' is defined by irregular menstrual periods or tuhrs, and a specialist must be consulted in this case.)

3.25 A tuhr can be complete while at the same time be invalid.

For example, after a menstrual period one has 15 days of tuhr, then 1 day of blood, then 15 days of tuhr, and then a menstrual period.

The 31 days of tuhr are complete but invalid because of the blood on day 16.

3.26 An invalid tuhr cannot be used as the habit, even though it might separate the two bleedings.

HABIT

3.27 All women are obligated to record their menstrual, lochial, and tuhr habits.

3.28 The menstrual habit is established by having a valid menstrual period and/or a valid tuhr once.

3.29 The lochial habit is established by having a valid lochia.

3.30 Only valid blood and valid tuhr can be used as the habit.

3.31 The menstrual beginner who does not have a valid menses or a valid tuhr and has continuous or irregular bleeding is given a 10-day menstrual habit and a 20-day tuhr habit.

3.32 The lochial beginner who does not have a valid lochia and has continuous bleeding is given a 40-day lochial habit.

3.33 The habit is used when there is an occurrence of invalid blood and/or invalid tuhr.

3.34 Change in habit occurs in either the place (def: 2.23) and/or number (def:2.24):

1. Change in the habitual place, i.e. the tuhr habit:

    1. If a woman does not see her menses at the expected time:

        For example, she has a 5-day menstrual habit and a 25-day tuhr habit.

        After 30 days of tuhr she has 5 days of menses.

    2. Or she sees it before the expected time but after a complete tuhr:

        For example, a woman has a 5-day menstrual habit and a 25-day tuhr habit.

        After 20 days of tuhr she has 5 days of menses.

        In the habitual place of her menses she has no blood.

2. Change in the habitual number, i.e. the menstrual habit:

    1. If a woman sees a different number of days that are valid blood;

    2. Or if the blood exceeds 10 days and a minimum occurs in the habitual place and the rest occurs in the tuhr:

        For example, a woman has a 5-day menstrual habit and 25-day tuhr habit.

        After 18 days of tuhr she has 11 days of blood and then a valid tuhr:

        1. The 7 days before the habitual place are istihada.

2. The 4 days in the habitual place are menses.
3. The menstrual habit has changed from 5 days to 4 days.

THE FORGOTTEN HABIT

3.35 A woman who does not know her habit (i.e. lost (mudalla) or confused (muhayyara)) and has constant or invalid bleeding, or an incomplete tuhr, must speak to a specialist in the rulings of menstruation and lochia.

THE BEGINNER

The menstrual or lochial beginner share similar rulings.

3.36 Any bleeding a beginner sees is either menses or lochia if the blood is valid and does not exceed the maximum.

3.37 Whenever the bleeding ends during the possible days of menstruation (i.e. after 72 hours), the beginner must take a purificatory bath (ghusl, def: 2.21), pray, and fast if Ramadan.

3.38 Whenever the bleeding ends during the possible days of lochia, the beginner must take a purificatory bath (ghusl), pray, and fast if Ramadan.

3.39 If the menstrual beginner sees blood for one hour, then 14 days of tuhr, and then an hour of blood, her habit is the first 10 days starting with the first hour of blood.

1. In this case, if it is Ramadan, she was not obliged to fast the 14 days of tuhr because she is still prepubescent.
2. The invalid tuhr joins the first blood with the second blood, and puberty is established.
3. She must make up the fast-days from day 1 to day 10 as they are legally considered menstruation.
4. She should have also taken a bath (ghusl) at the completion of day 10, from the time of the first blood.
5. If she did not take a bath (ghusl) at this time, then she must also make up the prayers until the time she did take a bath (ghusl).

6. The fasts of day 11 through day 14 are valid if she fasted them. The blood after day 14 is istihada (dysfunctional bleeding).

3.40 It is permissible to end menstruation with legal blood in the case of the menstrual beginner (dis: 11.70-71).

3.41 It is not permissible to begin menstruation with legal blood in the case of the menstrual beginner.

3.42 If the menstrual beginner sees blood for one hour, then 15 days or more of tuhr, then an hour of blood, then both bloods are istihada not menstruation.

3.43 If a lochial beginner after giving birth has 2 days of bleeding, then 37 days of tuhr, then spots for a day, her lochia is 40 days.

1. She now has established a lochial habit of 40 days.
2. If Ramadan came during those 37 days, she would have been required to fast.
3. However, because the last day of blood occurred during the possible days of lochia it caused all the days between the two bloods to be legal blood, (i.e. a mixed tuhr), which vitiates the fast.
4. Thus, she must make up all the days of Ramadan because she fasted them during legal lochia; however, there is no sin for her having fasted them.

3.44 Or if a lochial beginner after giving birth has 30 days of bleeding, then 14 days of tuhr, and then 1 day of blood. This legally makes the first 40 days lochia and the blood after day 44 istihada.

1. Her lochial habit is 40 days.
2. She goes back to her tuhr habit if she has one.
3. If she never had a valid tuhr, then her tuhr habit is 20 days.

3.45 Or if a lochial beginner has 30 days of bleeding, then 15 days of tuhr, and then 1 day of blood, in this case, her lochial habit is 30 days and the blood after the 15-day tuhr is menses if it completes the minimum (72 hours).

A WOMAN WITH A HABIT

3.46 If a woman has a habit and sees that which matches her habit, then it stays the same.

3.47 If a woman sees blood or tuhr different from her habit, then her habit changes if they are valid.

3.48 If either the blood or tuhr is invalid, a woman returns to her habit and the excess blood is istihada.

3.49 It is permissible to begin and/or end menstruation with legal blood (dis: 11.70-71).

3.50 A woman stops ritual prayer whenever:

1. She sees blood after a complete tuhr;
2. Or she sees blood in excess of her habit in the possible days of menstruation or lochia;
3. Or she sees blood prior to her menstrual habit such that if these early days are added to her habit, the total does not exceed the maximum (240 hours).

   For example, a woman has a 7-day menstrual habit and a 25-day tuhr habit.

   1. She sees blood after 22 days of tuhr, i.e. 3 days before the habit.
   2. In this case adding these 3 early days to the 7 habitual days does not exceed the maximum.

4. Or as soon as she sees blood prior to her menstrual habit such that the remainder of the tuhr consists of a minimal menstruation and a valid tuhr.

   For example, a woman with a 3-day menstrual habit and a 40-day tuhr habit sees blood after 20 days of tuhr.

   1. She is obliged to stop ritual prayer and fast.
   2. The blood she sees after day 20, if it reaches 3 days, is menses because it is preceded by a valid tuhr.
   3. After these 3 days of menses there would be a valid tuhr of 17 days. Therefore, it separates the two bloods: the blood after day 20 and the blood after day 40.
   4. The menstrual habit is applied if the blood exceeds the maximum; it returns to the 3-day menstrual habit followed by a 17-day complete tuhr.

(Dis: 11.51-53.)

COLORS OF BLOOD

3.51 The colors of blood are:

1. black: very dark heavy red blood that usually clots and seems as if it is almost black;
2. red;
3. brown;
4. green;
5. yellow;
6. dusky or a trace of color that is not pure white.

In other words, all non-white or non-clear discharge is legally considered blood.

3.52 (*t*: Any discharge, white, clear or colored, caused by an infection (dis: 15.1-24), illness, or operation is impure (najis) and nullifies ablution and is not considered menses or lochia.)

NORMAL VAGINAL DISCHARGE

3.53 (*t*: The colors of normal vaginal discharge (tuhr):

1. White: the texture could be creamy or liquid.
2. Clear: transparent or cloudy. The texture can be sticky like raw egg whites during the time of ovulation, and like saliva at other times.

It is normal at various times in one's cycle that there is no discharge (dis: 15.1-4).)

3.54 The color of normal vaginal discharge is only considered after the immediate removal of the kursuf (def: 2.20) and the discharge is fresh, as it tends to turn yellow as it oxidizes.

(*t*: Pads or pantiliners may be used during menses or lochia. However, one cannot depend on them to determine the color of discharge as they are placed far from the vaginal opening. The kursuf must be used properly (dis: 5.1) to determine the color.)

3.55 If the discharge changes color after being exposed for a while, the change in color is not considered.

1. If the discharge comes out white and oxidizes or dries and turns yellow or dusky, the color is not considered.
2. If the discharge comes out yellow and dries white, the yellow is considered.

3.56 Yellow discharge is impure (najis) and invalidates ablution.

3.57 White residue that dries yellow is pure.

3.58 (*t*: If a female has fresh yellow discharge most of the month, then she should see a doctor or health practitioner. (dis: 15.1-42).

Again, keep in mind that the color and its legal ruling are from fresh discharge and not the dry residue of it.

Warning: a virgin should not permit a doctor to give her an internal vaginal examination. Many doctors in the West, generally speaking, do not consider a girl's virginity relevant or important. If such an examination is absolutely necessary, it should be done in consultation with a religious Muslim doctor.)

3.59 (*t*: Normal vaginal discharge (tuhr) is pure and does not nullify ablution according to Imam Abu Hanifa.

His two companions, Abu Yusuf and Mohammad, consider it impure (najis) and that it nullifies ablution.

Ibn 'Abidin states that the authorized position is that of the Imam Abu Hanifa; see *Hashiya* 1.555, 2.339, 2.456 for the discussion of their differences of opinion.)

4

Onset of Valid Bleeding

Onset of Menstruation

4.1 The onset of menstruation occurs with the exiting of blood from the vagina or it reaching the edge of the vagina, just as urine invalidates ablution if it reaches the edge of the urethra.

4.2 Menstruation is legally established if the bleeding is from a female of 9 lunar years or older.

4.3 If a woman feels as if the blood is coming down but it does not exit or reach the edge of the vagina, or she uses something to block it from exiting, then there is no legal ruling for it. It does not take the ruling of menstruation until the blood exits.

4.4 However, if a woman blocks the blood after it has once come out, then the state of menstruation remains. This is not true for the state of istihada.

4.5 If a woman in tuhr places a kursuf correctly and later sees blood, menstruation begins when she sees the blood, not at the time she placed the kursuf.

4.6 Bleeding caused by medication during the possible days of menstruation is menstruation.

Onset of Lochia

4.7 Lochia begins with the bleeding after 'most of the baby' has been delivered.

4.8 'Most' of the baby means if head first, then after the chest comes out; if feet first, then after the navel comes out.

4.9 'Baby' means from the stage of a fetus with some discernible human features such as finger, hand, or hair and so forth, to a full-term fetus.

4.10 One is obliged to pray until 'most of the baby' has been delivered i.e. during labor.

a) (*t*: If one is unable to make ablution alone, then one may seek help to make it.)

b) If unable to make ablution, then one makes tayammum.

c) (*t*: If one is unable to dress, then one may cover with a sheet.)

d) If unable to pray standing, then one prays sitting.

e) If unable to pray sitting, then one prays on one's side or back moving one's head.

f) (*t*: If completely unable to pray, then those prayers missed must be recorded and made up after the lochia.)

4.11 If a woman has a dry birth (*t*: a birth without any lochia), she is required to take a purificatory bath (ghusl) and pray immediately.

MULTIPLE BIRTHS

4.12 For multiple births, lochia begins with the first delivery as long as there is not an interval of 6 months between the deliveries.

CAESARIAN BIRTH

4.13 If a woman has a caesarian section, then only the blood exiting from the vagina is lochia.

4.14 If blood exits from the incision, and no blood exits from the vagina, then she has no lochia.

MISCARRIAGE

4.15 If the miscarried fetus shows any human features (def: 4.9), then the bleeding after the miscarriage is lochia.

4.16 Bleeding after a miscarried embryo (i.e. the stage before any discernible human features) is not lochia.

4.17 If the embryo has no discernible human features, then the bleeding before and/or after the miscarriage is menstruation if it continues for at least 3 days (72 hours) and is preceded by a complete tuhr; otherwise, it is istihada (dis: 11.46, 11.82-84 and Menstrual Case 14).

4.18 (Ibn 'Abidin): A miscarried fetus or a stillbirth (i.e. a baby that dies before or during delivery) is:

a) named;
b) washed;
c) wrapped in a clean cloth and not shrouded;
d) buried but not prayed over.

4.19 An embryo that has no discernible human features (def:4.9) is:

a) named;
b) washed;
c) wrapped in a cloth;
d) buried but not prayed over.

4.20 The placenta, umbilical cord, and amniotic sac are wrapped in a cloth and buried.

(*Hashiya* 5.2.35-36, 5.313-14)

5

THE KURSUF

RULINGS FOR THE KURSUF

5.1 The kursuf (def:2.20) is placed between the labia minora (the inner lips) at the opening of the vagina.

(*t:* Usually cotton cloth, cotton wool, or paper tissue is used as a kursuf.

Pads or pantiliners may be used during menses or lochia. However, they are not considered kursufs as they are not placed at the opening of the vagina. One cannot depend on them to determine the end of menses or lochia. If one is having difficulty verifying the end, then the kursuf—used properly—can confirm the end.)

5.2 A kursuf is placed either *at* the opening of the vagina for normal use or completely inside the vagina (dis: 5.4) like a tampon during istihada (dysfunctional bleeding) for non-virgins (dis 5.7).

5.3 It is sunna for a virgin to use it during her menstruation.

5.4 It is not permissible for a virgin under any circumstances to place the whole kursuf in the vagina (as in using a tampon).

(*t:* Inserting a kursuf completely inside the vagina could break the hymen causing a virgin to become a non-virgin, even though some tampon companies claim otherwise.)

5.5 It is recommended at all times for the non-virgin.

5.6 It is not permissible to insert the whole kursuf into the vagina (as in using a tampon) for a non-virgin during her menses, lochia, or tuhr.

5.7 Inserting the whole kursuf into the vagina is recommended in the case of a non-virgin with istihada if it does not harm or irritate her.

(*t:* A tampon should not be left in too long as this could cause Toxic Shock Syndrome (dis:15.37-42). There are alternatives to tampons on the market.)

EXITING OF BLOOD

5.8 If the kursuf is placed at the opening of the vagina and gets wet with blood, menstruation begins, or in the case of istihada (dysfunctional bleeding), ablution is nullified.

BLOCKING THE BLOOD

5.9 If the kursuf is placed inside the vagina and is completely wet, but no blood comes out or reaches the edge of the vaginal opening, then menses does not legally begin until the kursuf is removed or until the blood leaks out.

5.10 In the case of istihada, if she makes ablution after inserting the kursuf as long as the blood does not leak or reach the edge of the vaginal opening, then ablution is valid.

(*t:* Any colored discharge coming down the string of a tampon is considered leakage, and it nullifies ablution (dis: 9.1-38).

5.11 (*t:* One should also be aware that placing the whole kursuf inside the vagina vitiates the fast.

If she wishes to fast and has a need to insert the kursuf, she can place it inside the vagina before Fajr (dawn) and remove it right after Maghrib (sunset). This should only be done when absolutely necessary and when the daytime hours are not very long because of the possibility of infection (dis: 15.37-42). Other methods might be less dangerous, such as using a diaphragm to block the istihada.)

6

END OF VALID BLEEDING

ASCERTAINING THE END

6.1 Any colored discharge is considered blood (dis:3.51).

6.2 Until the discharge is white or clear, or there is no discharge at all, menses or lochia has not ended.

6.3 The kursuf must be placed correctly between the labia minora (the inner lips) at the opening of the vagina when used to determine any legal rulings (dis: 5.1).

6.4 (*t*: For women with problems, using the kursuf to determine the end of their menses or lochia is helpful. While pads or pantiliners may be used, one cannot depend on them to determine the end of menses or lochia as they are placed far from the opening of the vagina.)

6.5 The Sacred Law does not require a woman to check herself frequently, nor is she expected to insert anything inside to determine if the bleeding has stopped (this applies to non-virgins, as inserting anything for virgins is unlawful).

6.6 When the end is pending, she is obliged to check the kursuf—which must have been placed correctly—before the end of the prayer time such that she has time to take a bath (ghusl, def: 2.21) and pray the prayer in its preferred time (def: 2.22).

6.7 The color of the discharge is determined immediately after the kursuf—which must have been placed correctly—is removed and the discharge is fresh. Any change in color after this time is not considered, as we have mentioned the legal ruling is from the fresh discharge and not its oxidized or dried residue.

6.8 If a woman during menses or lochia places a clean kursuf—which must have been placed correctly—at night and goes to sleep, then wakes up to find the kursuf clean or has a white or clear discharge on it, her menstruation or lochia ended from the time she placed the kursuf—not the time she sees it.

In this example, if she places it at 'Isha' (nightfall) and wakes up at Fajr (dawn), she must make up 'Isha' and *witr* prayers before she prays the Fajr prayer.

In contrast, if a woman in tuhr places a kursuf and later sees blood, menstruation begins when she sees the blood, not when she placed the kursuf.

AT THE MAXIMUM

6.9 If the blood stops at the maximum (240 hours), then her menstruation or lochia has legally ended.

6.10 In the specific cases of ending at the maximum, it is permissible for the husband to have sexual intercourse with his wife before the purificatory bath (ghusl) even though this is disliked.

6.11 If there is enough time left of a prayer time to say 'Allah' of 'Allahu Akbar', (i.e. the opening of the prayer), then she is required to make up that prayer after her bath (ghusl).

6.12 If the menses stop just before Fajr (dawn) in Ramadan, her fast is valid—even though she has not taken a bath (ghusl)—and she needs to make up 'Isha' (nightfall) and *witr* prayers before she prays Fajr.

6.13 The last part of the prayer time determines if one is qualified to pray or one has to make it up, or qualified to fast or not.

(*t*: For example, 'Asr (midafternoon) prayer comes in at 3:05 p.m. and her menses end at 3:00 p.m.

In this case, where her bleeding ends at the maximum, her bath (ghusl) takes her into the time of 'Asr; however, she must make up that Dhuhr (noon) before she prays 'Asr.)

BEFORE THE MAXIMUM

6.14 One is required to make up the prayer if there is enough time before the next prayer time to take a bath (ghusl) and say 'Allah' of the prayer opening 'Allahu Akbar', or the time it takes to make tayammum if she qualifies for it.

6.15 The time it takes to have a purificatory bath (ghusl) is considered part of the menstrual or lochial period.

6.16 If there is not enough time after the blood stops to take a bath (ghusl) and say 'Allah' of 'Allahu Akbar', then she is not required to make up that prayer.

(*t*: For example, the 'Asr (midafternoon) prayer time comes in at 3:05 p.m. and her menses end at 3:00 p.m. before the maximum.

1. The last part of the prayer time is what determines if one is qualified for prayer or not. In this case her bath (ghusl) takes her into the 'Asr time thus making her unqualified to pray Dhuhr (noon).
2. Therefore she is not required to make up that noon prayer.)

6.17 If there is not enough time after the blood stops to take a bath (ghusl) and say 'Allah' of 'Allahu Akbar' before Fajr (dawn) in Ramadan, then her fast is invalid and she must make it up.

6.18 If the blood stops just before Fajr in Ramadan and her bath (ghusl) goes into the time of Fajr, then her fast that day is invalid.

6.19 One of the stipulations of fasting is being free of menses or lochia, and until the bath (ghusl) is made, one is not free of either of these states.

6.20 After taking her bath (ghusl) after Fajr, she is not permitted to eat during the day because of the sacredness of the month, and she must make up this fast-day.

(*t*: For example, it is Ramadan and her menstruation ends as usual on day 7 at 5:00 am and Fajr comes in at 5:03 am.

1. There is not enough time for her to undress, warm up the water and take her bath (ghusl) before Fajr comes in.
2. The bath (ghusl) will go a few minutes into Fajr time, thus making her fast that day invalid. She is not required to make up the 'Isha' (nightfall) prayer because she was not qualified to pray at the end of its time.

3. A similar but opposite situation is if her menses begin just a few minutes before Maghrib (sunset), which would vitiate the fast.)

6.21 Sexual intercourse is unlawful until one of the following occurs:

1. A woman takes a bath (ghusl);
2. or she is qualified to make tayammum (dry ablution) and does so and prays any obligatory or nafl prayer;
3. or a complete prayer time expires and she has not prayed. In other words, that prayer becomes a debt that she must make up.

   For example, if menses or lochia stops at sunrise, sexual intercourse is unlawful until the 'Asr (midafternoon) prayer time comes in because that would mean she owes the Dhuhr (noon) prayer.

   Or if menses or lochia stops just as 'Isha' is coming in, then sexual intercourse is unlawful until the time of Fajr.

6.22 Sexual intercourse is permissible after the bath (ghusl) if the blood stops at the established menstrual or lochial habit or after the habit.

6.23 Sexual intercourse is unlawful if the blood stops before the established menstrual or lochial habit, even though she is required to pray and fast if Ramadan.

(*t*: This prohibition of sexual intercourse also applies to a non-Muslim wife if the blood stops before the established habit.)

6.24 If the blood stops before the habit, sexual intercourse is permissible only after she reaches her habit (dis 14.8).

(*t*: For example, the menstrual habit is 9 days.

1. This month the blood stops on day 5.
2. She is required to take a bath (ghusl), pray, and fast, but sexual intercourse is unlawful until day 9, the end of her habit.)

This is the same for lochia if it stops before the lochial habit.

6.25 Every time the blood stops during the possible days of menstruation within the first 3 days, she is required to wait until the end of the prayer time to see if she must pray or not.

1. If the blood does not return then she makes ablution and prays.
2. She continues her fast or refrains from eating if it is Ramadan.
3. If the blood returns, then she does not pray or fast.

6.26 Every time the blood stops during the possible days of menstruation but after the first 3 days and before her habit, she is required to wait until the end of the prayer time to see whether or not she must pray.

If the blood does not return, she takes her bath (ghusl) and prays in the proper time (i.e. at the end of the preferred prayer time and before the disliked time (def: 2.22)).

6.27 Every time the blood stops after the first 3 days, before or after her habit, during the possible days of menstruation, she is required to take a bath (ghusl) and start her obligatory worship.

6.28 All of the previous rulings are the same for lochia except that every time the blood stops during the possible days of lochia, she is required to take a bath (ghusl).

6.29 The purificatory bath (ghusl) for menstruation or lochia is the same for major ritual impurity (janaba).

6.30 A non-Muslim female married to a Muslim is not required to take a purificatory bath (ghusl). She enters her tuhr interval with the end of either menses or lochia. Her Muslim husband is responsible for knowing the Sacred Law rulings on menstruation and lochia.

BEFORE THE HABIT

6.31 Whenever menstrual or lochial bleeding stops, a purificatory bath (ghusl) is obligatory.

6.32 If the bleeding ends prior to her normal habit, then she is obliged to wait until the end of the prayer time, such that if the bleeding ends she has enough time to take a bath (ghusl) and pray in the preferred prayer time (def: 2.22).

6.33 Sexual intercourse is unlawful if the bleeding stops before the completion of the menstrual/lochial habit because of the strong possibility of the blood returning according to its habit (dis 14.8). However, she is required to pray and fast.

AFTER THE HABIT

6.34 If the bleeding exceeds her habit but is less than the maximum, she takes a bath (ghusl) and prays when the blood stops.

6.35 If the bleeding completes the maximum, then the purificatory bath (ghusl) is immediately obligatory, and all bleeding after the maximum is istihada (dysfunctional vaginal bleeding).

6.36 If the blood exceeds 240 hours and there is a menstrual habit, the days in excess of the habit are istihada.

1. She must make up the prayers omitted during the days in excess of her habit.
2. There is no sin for having not performed the prayers as she is obliged to wait as long as there is bleeding during the possible days of menstruation.

6.37 As long as there is bleeding during the possible days of menstruation or lochia, a woman must wait until it stops or it reaches the maximum.

(*t*: For example, a woman has a 7-day menstrual habit but this month she bleeds until day 12.

a) She must wait until day 10 and then take a bath (ghusl).

b) As soon as she sees that the blood exceeds the maximum (240 hours), she needs to make up the prayers of the days over her habit.

c) In this case, she makes up the prayers for day 8, day 9, and day 10.)

TIME OF THE PURIFICATORY BATH (GHUSL)

6.38 The time to complete the minimal purificatory bath (ghusl, dis: 2.21) is considered part of the menstrual or lochial period if it ends *before* the maximum. (*t*: It takes approximateley 15 minutes in these modern times under normal circumstances.)

6.39 The time of the purificatory bath (ghusl) is not considered part of the menstrual or lochial period if it ends at the maximum.

(*t*: For those interested in a detailed explanation see *al-Kasani's Bada'i al-Sana'i fi Tartib al-Shara'i* 1.267.)

MENOPAUSE

6.40 When a woman reaches the age of 55 lunar years (53 solar years and 4 months), she is regarded as having reached menopause if she no longer has menstrual periods.

6.41 However, if she is 55 or older and she still has valid blood, it is menstruation. Otherwise, it is istihada (dysfunctional bleeding).

6.42 (t: Hormone replacement therapy (HRT) causes bleeding. The blood is valid and is considered menstruation if it is the same as her pre-menopausal menses. Otherwise, it is istihada.)

7

CHANGE IN HABIT

7.1 (*t:* It is normal that a menstrual period or tuhr interval fluctuates within the legal boundaries. The changes in these situations are usually predictable. As long as the blood and/or tuhr is within the legal realms, then changes are valid.)

7.2 (*t:* Problems occur when either blood or tuhr is invalid. This is the reason it is obligatory to record the menstrual, lochial, and tuhr habits.)

7.3 (*t:* In solving a problem, one first tries to apply the habitual place (zaman, def: 2.23) and the habitual number ('adad, def: 2.24) if possible. If not, the place takes precedence over the number. If the place is not applicable, then the number is used.)

7.4 (*t:* It is in the cases of invalid blood and/or invalid tuhr that habits are needed and used.

There are many examples of legal blood and legal tuhr where the ruling changes from day to day during and after the possible days of menstruation or lochia.

Knowing if one should pray or not, fast or not, or make up prayers or not, is determined by the recorded bloods and tuhrs (dis: 11.1).

See 'Lochial Case Studies' and 'Menstrual Case Studies,' for detailed examples of various problems.)

BLOOD EXCEEDING THE MAXIMUM

7.5 When bleeding exceeds 10 days, the place of the habit takes precedence if the bleeding reaches the minimum (72 hours) in the habitual place.

7.6 If there is bleeding during the possible days, a woman cannot pray or fast, but as soon as that same blood exceeds the maximum (240 hours), then all the days in excess of the habit become istihada (dysfunctional bleeding).

(*t*: For example, a woman with a 7-day menstrual habit bleeds over the maximum.

a) She must wait until the bleeding stops or she reaches the maximum, whichever comes first.

b) In this case, the blood does not stop and she waits until it reaches the maximum; at which time, she must take a bath (ghusl).

c) Now that the bleeding has exceeded the maximum, she knows that all the blood in excess of her habit becomes istihada.

d) She must make up the prayers of each day over her habit, that is day 8, day 9, and day 10.

e) She has no sin for omitting these prayers because she is obliged to wait until the maximum, but she would be sinning if she does not make them up.)

7.7 When the bleeding exceeds the maximum and there is no minimum in the habitual place, the place changes but the number remains the same from when the first blood occurred.

For example, a woman sees 11 days of blood not in her habitual place or she sees less than 3 days in the proper place, then her menstruation has changed in regards to the place in the month but not the number of days.

In this case, her habit is the first 5 days of the month.

a) She sees 11 days of blood starting on day 4 of the month.

b) The days of blood concurring with her habitual place are day 4 and day 5 which is less than the minimum.

c) Thus, her menstruation starts from day 4 of the month but will last like the original habit of 5 days.

7.8 When the bleeding exceeds the maximum and there is a minimum in the habitual place, then that which occurs in the habitual place is menses and the rest is istihada.

For example, a woman sees 11 days of blood of which 3 days are concurrent with her habit of 5 days:

a) Then her new habit is 3 days and the rest is istihada. In this case, the bleeding starts 2 days later than the expected habit and lasts for 11 days.

b) The 3 days of blood that concur with the habit are day 3, day 4, and day 5 of the habit.

c) Thus, her habit has changed from 5 days to 3 days because the 3 days are in the proper place and the blood exceeds the maximum.

7.9 When the bleeding exceeds the maximum and the number of days concurs with her habit, the habit remains.

(*t*: For example, a woman sees 11 days of blood, of which 7 days concur with her habit of 7 days:

a) The 7 days are menses and the rest is istihada.

b) Her menses start at the habitual time and exceeds the maximum (10 days).

c) The first 7 days are menses and the 3 extra days are istihada.

d) But she only realizes this after the completion of day 10 and sees that the blood is continuing.

e) Thus, she takes a bath (ghusl) at the completion of 10 days and makes up the prayer for day 8, day 9, and day 10.

f) However, if she only sees 10 days of blood, which is valid, her menstrual habit changes from 7 days to 10 days.)

(Dis: Precepts 36 – 39.)

BLOOD NOT EXCEEDING THE MAXIMUM

7.10 If the bleeding does not exceed the maximum, then all of it is menses if she has a valid tuhr after it.

For example, a woman has a menstrual habit of 5 days and tuhr habit of 25 days. She sees 6 days of blood, and then a valid tuhr.

The habit changes to a 6-day menstrual habit.

CHANGE OF LOCHIAL HABIT

7.11 If blood exceeds 40 days, then the habit remains and the bleeding exceeding the habit is istihada (dysfunctional bleeding).

(*t*: This is realized after the completion of the 40 days.)

7.12 She must wait until the bleeding either stops or completes 40 days (960 hours).

7.13 Upon exceeding day 40, she makes up the prayers of the days that are in excess of her habit.

(*t*: For example, a woman has a 30-day lochial habit and during this lochia she continues to see blood until day 41.

a) She must wait until the completion of day 40, though she continues to see blood, she immediately takes her purificatory bath (ghusl).

b) She must make up the prayers from day 31 to day 40.)

7.14 If a woman sees more or less than her habit but within the possible days of lochia, then what she sees is her new habit as long as there is a valid tuhr after it.

(*t*: For example, the lochial habit is 30 days, and she sees blood for 35 days. Then her new habit is 35 days.

Or her habit is 30 days, and the bleeding stops at day 25. Then her new habit is 25 days.)

(*t*: The 'Lochial Case Studies' and 'Menstrual Case Studies' sections have detailed examples of various types of lochial, menstrual and tuhr problems and changes.)

8

Constant Bleeding

(*t:* Istihada (dysfunctional vaginal bleeding) in the books of Sacred Law usually refers to constant bleeding (dis: 9.1-38). However, constant bleeding could be non-stop, intermittent, or spotting.

When invalid blood is confirmed, many of the rulings are revised; for this reason keeping a record of all blood is essential. See '*Revision of the Day-by-Day Rulings*' in the 'Lochial Case Studies' and 'Menstrual Case Studies' sections for details of how blood can first be considered valid but then verified as invalid.)

A Woman with a Habit

8.1 If a woman with a menstrual habit has constant bleeding, then she returns to her habit in regard to both menstruation and tuhr, if the tuhr habit is less than 6 months.

8.2 If the tuhr exceeds 6 months, then the habit is made 6 months minus one hour while the menstrual habit remains the same in regard to the postmarital waiting period ('idda).

8.3 (*t:* If a woman with a lochial habit has constant bleeding after childbirth, she returns to her lochial, tuhr, and menstrual habits (dis: Menstrual Case Thirteen).

The Beginner

8.4 If a menstrual beginner has constant bleeding (*t:* for example, she has 30 days of non-stop bleeding), then the first 10 days are menses and the following 20 days are legal tuhr. This is her habit.

8.5 If a lochial beginner, who has never had a menstrual period, has constant blood after giving birth, her lochia is the first 40 days. This is followed by 20 days of legal tuhr, and then 10 days of menses.

1. She is given a 40-day lochial habit, a 20-day tuhr habit, and a 10-day menstrual habit.
2. As long as she has constant bleeding she applies this 10-day menstrual habit and 20-day tuhr habit.

8.6 (*t*: A woman who is a lochial beginner with constant bleeding and has a menstrual habit is given a 40-day lochia and returns to her menstrual habit and tuhr habit.)

VALID BLOOD AND VALID TUHR

8.7 If a menstrual beginner has valid blood and a valid tuhr, then has constant bleeding, she is considered a woman with a habit and returns to this habit.

For example, she sees 5 days of blood, 40 days of tuhr, and then constant bleeding.

1. From the time of the constant blood, the first 5 days is menses and the next 40 days tuhr.
2. This is her habit and it is repeated as long as there is constant bleeding.
3. During the days of legal tuhr, she is obliged to pray, and fast if Ramadan, and sexual intercourse is permissible.

INVALID BLOOD AND INVALID TUHR

8.8 If a menstrual beginner sees invalid blood and has an invalid tuhr, they cannot be taken as the habit.

8.9 If the tuhr is incomplete, then the time of the first blood to the time of constant bleeding is considered legal blood.

For example, she sees 11 days of blood, then 14 days of tuhr, and then constant bleeding.

1. The time of the first blood is considered the start of the constant blood.
2. The first 10 days are menses, then the next 20 days legal tuhr.

3. She follows this 10-day menstrual habit and 20-day tuhr habit as long as she has constant bleeding.

8.10 When the tuhr is complete but the menstrual period plus the tuhr interval does not exceed 30 days, she is given a 10-day menstrual habit and a 20-day tuhr habit.

For example, a menstrual beginner sees 11 days of blood, then 15 days of tuhr, and then constant bleeding.

1. The first 10 days are menses, and then 20 days of tuhr (i.e. the 16 days of tuhr plus the first 4 days of the constant blood).
2. From the time of the constant blood, the first 4 days are legal tuhr.
3. From day 5 of the constant blood, a 10-day menstrual habit and 20-day tuhr is applied.
4. This is her habit as long as the constant blood continues.

8.11 When the tuhr is complete but the menstrual period plus the tuhr interval exceeds 30 days, she complies with the tuhr for as long as it lasts. Then when the constant blood begins she is given a 10-day menstrual habit and a 20-day tuhr habit.

For example, a menstrual beginner sees 11 days of blood, then 20 days of tuhr, and then has constant bleeding.

1. The first 10 days are menses, followed by 21 days of invalid tuhr.
2. From the time of constant bleeding, the first 10 days are menses and the next 20 days are legal tuhr.
3. This is her habit as long as the constant blood continues.
4. Even though the 21 days are a complete tuhr, it is invalid because the first day is blood, and consequently cannot be used as the habit.

Valid Blood and Invalid Tuhr

8.12 When the blood is valid and the tuhr invalid, the valid blood is taken as the menstrual habit.

For example, a menstrual beginner sees 3 days of blood, then 15 days of tuhr, then 1 day of blood, then 15 days of tuhr, and then constant bleeding.

1. The first 3 days are menses and 31 days are tuhr.

2. From the time of the constant bleeding, the first 3 days are menses and 27 days are tuhr.

8.13 However, if the second 15 days of tuhr were only 14 days, then the first 15 days of tuhr would be a valid tuhr.

1. Then the 1 day of blood plus the 14 days of tuhr are legal blood, of which the first 3 days are menstruation, and the following 12 days are tuhr.

2. From the onset of the constant blood, the first 3 days are added to the 12 previous days to make up the total days of the tuhr habit.

3. After which the next 3 days are menstruation.

4. She has a 3-day menstrual habit and a 15-day tuhr habit.

5. In this case, the very first blood and tuhr are valid and are used as the habit.

PUBERTY THROUGH PREGNANCY

8.14 If a menstrual beginner sees 15 days of tuhr, then constant bleeding, this could only happen in the case where this beginner reaches puberty by being pregnant and never had menses before pregnancy.

For example, she has 40 days of lochia, then 15 days of tuhr, and then constant bleeding.

1. From the start of the constant bleeding, the first 10 days are menses, and the next 15 days tuhr.

2. This is her habit as long as the constant blood continues.

3. And if the tuhr is more than 15 days, it is valid and would be used as the habit.

8.15 If the lochial beginner has blood exceeding 40 days, then 15 days or more of tuhr, and then has constant bleeding, the blood in excess of the 40 days makes the 15 days or more an invalid tuhr. It cannot be used as a habit.

She is given a lochial habit of 40 days, then 20 days of legal tuhr, and then 10 days of menses. As long as she has constant blood she applies the 10-day menstrual habit and 20-day tuhr habit.

8.16 Another scenario is when the blood exceeds 40 days, there are 20 days or more of tuhr, and then there is constant bleeding.

From the time of the constant bleeding, the first 10 days are menses and the next 20 days tuhr, and that is her habit as long as she has constant bleeding.

9

Chronic Annulment of Ablution

9.1 The cause of chronic annulment of ablution, such as istihada (dysfunctional vaginal bleeding), continually breaking wind, urinary incontinence, and fecal incontinence, is referred to as the *excuse* ('udhr).

9.2 The person suffering from chronic annulment of ablution is referred to as the *excused* (ma'dhur).

9.3 If the state of minor ritual impurity (annulment of ablution) is caused by something constant that continues for a complete prescribed prayer time, such that there is not enough time to make ablution and pray, then this qualifies as an *excuse* and it qualifies the person as an *excused*.

9.4 Someone who qualifies as an *excused* person is exempt from maintaining the normal state of ritual purity that is stipulated in regard to certain types of worship.

9.5 (*t*: All references to prayer times are to prescribed prayer times. The prescribed prayer times are five:

1. Dhuhr (noon) to 'Asr (midafternoon);
2. 'Asr to Maghrib (sunset);
3. Maghrib to 'Isha' (nightfall);
4. 'Isha' to Fajr (dawn);
5. Fajr to sunrise.)

9.6 (*t*: The interval between sunrise and noon is a non-prescribed prayer time; rulings for chronic annulment of ablution during this time are contingent on one's status at the end of the Dhuhr.

For example, if one cuts one's finger at 10 A.M. and the bleeding persists into the Dhuhr prayer time, then one must wait for the bleeding to stop to pray the Dhuhr prayer. Or if the bleeding continues, then one must wait until the end of the Dhuhr prayer time such that there is enough time to make ablution and pray before the time expires (dis: 9.12).)

EXCUSED STATUS

9.7 The *excused* status is established when an *excuse* (def: 9.1) continues for a complete prayer time; it is cancelled when the *excuse* ceases for a complete prayer time.

9.8 If the *excuse* ceases for a complete prayer time, then one loses the *excused* status from the time it ceased.

9.9 After the *excuse* is established, it is not conditional that it be active for the complete prayer time. It is enough to see it once each prayer time.

9.10 Ablution made for the *excuse* is not nullified by the recurrence of the *excuse*, except when that prescribed prayer time expires. During that specific prayer time, one may pray any amount of obligatory and non-obligatory prayers, as well as performing any other worship that requires ritual purity such as reading the Qur'an. Conditions for the validity of this ablution are:

a) ablution is made because of the *excuse* and not another reason;

b) ablution is made in the prayer time and not before it.

This ablution remains valid during that specific prayer time, whether the ablution is made while the *excuse* is active or it becomes active after the ablution.

LOSING THE EXCUSED STATUS

9.11 A prayer prayed with the *excused* status must be re-prayed if in the:

a) first prayer time: the *excuse* ceases during ablution or during the prayer before the final sitting;

b) second prayer time: cessation continues for the complete prayer time;

c) third prayer time: time comes in;

In this case, the prayer of the first time must be repeated.

(*t*: For example, if the *excuse* ceases while praying Dhuhr (noon) and does not return during 'Asr (midafternoon) and Maghrib (sunset) comes in, then one is obliged to re-pray that Dhuhr prayer.

a) The *excused* status is cancelled because the *excuse* ceases for a complete prayer time, i.e. the second prayer time.

b) Hence, the *excused* status ended in the first prayer time.

c) In this case, the *excuse* status ended in the Dhuhr prayer time; that Dhuhr prayer was performed with minor ritual impurity but this is only established after the fact.

d) That Dhuhr prayer is re-prayed in this Maghrib prayer time; the required prayer order is waived.

e) If the *excuse* becomes active before the end of the second prayer time, then one does not repeat the prayer of the first prayer time.)

SHORT OF THE EXCUSED STATUS

9.12 If a prayer time comes in and one has not prayed yet and chronic annulment of ablution starts and persists, one must wait until the end of that prayer time such that there is only enough time to make ablution and pray. Then one makes ablution and prays before the prayer time expires. If the chronic annulment of ablution ceases during the second prayer time, one must repeat the prayer prayed at the end of the previous prayer time. If the chronic annulment of ablution continues through the second prayer time, one does not repeat the prayer because the *excuse* is established from the time it started.

(*t*: For example, chronic annulment of ablution starts after the Dhuhr (noon) prayer time comes in, and one has not prayed Dhuhr yet.

a) If chronic annulment of ablution persists, then one waits until the end of the prayer time to make ablution and pray.

b) If it stops before the 'Asr (midafternoon) prayer time expires, then one is obliged to re-pray that Dhuhr prayer.

A situation might be that during the Dhuhr prayer time before having prayed, one cuts one's finger and it bleeds.

a) One must wait until the end of the Dhuhr prayer time to pray while the finger is still bleeding.

b) 'Asr prayer time comes in and the finger is spotting blood, and then completely stops during that prayer time; the *excused* status is not established.

c) The Dhuhr prayer is repeated because it was prayed with minor ritual impurity given that there is no *excused* status.

d) Here, one expects the bleeding will stop and it does in the 'Asr prayer time; one re-prays the Dhuhr prayer and then prays the 'Asr prayer.

When there is hope that the cause of chronic annulment of ablution will stop before the preferred prayer time ends, then one should delay praying that prayer as in this case of the 'Asr prayer.)

ACTIVE AND NON-ACTIVE EXCUSE

9.13 If ablution is made for the *excuse*, then it is valid for the rest of the prayer time.

(*t*: For example, an *excused* person has ablution but it gets nullified due to using the lavatory.

a) A new ablution is made due to using the lavatory, and meanwhile the *excuse* is not and has not been active; ablution is nullified when the *excuse* becomes active.

b) Then, this person makes ablution because of the *excuse*.

c) This ablution made because of the *excuse* is valid until the end of the prayer time if it is not nullified by another reason.)

9.14 If the *excuse* is active during or after ablution, then ablution is nullified when the prayer time expires.

9.15 Despite the fact of having the *excused* status, if the *excuse* is not active while making ablution for a reason other than the *excuse* and afterwards it becomes active, then ablution is nullified even if the prayer time has not expired because the ablution was for other than the *excuse*.

9.16 If the *excuse* is not active after making ablution for a reason other than the *excuse*, then it is not nullified even if the prayer time expires.

9.17 If one makes ablution because of the *excuse* and something else occurs that nullifies it, then ablution is nullified immediately.

9.18 If the *excuse* is not active during or after one makes ablution and nothing else nullifies it, then the ablution is valid even if the prayer time expires until the *excuse* or something else nullifies it.

9.19 If one makes ablution because of blood flowing from one nostril and after ablution blood flows from the other nostril, then ablution is nullified.

9.20 If blood is flowing from both nostrils while one makes ablution, then blood from one of the nostrils stops, ablution is not nullified until the prayer time expires.

9.21 Smallpox and pustules are multiple abscesses. If one makes ablution while some of the abscesses are not excreting pus and after ablution they excrete pus, then ablution is nullified immediately, even if the prayer time has not expired.

9.22 If one makes ablution while all the abscesses are excreting pus, then ablution is not nullified until the prayer time expires.

9.23 If an *excused* person makes ablution without a need to and the *excuse* becomes active, then ablution is nullified.

For example, if an *excused* person makes ablution and:

a) the *excuse* is not active;

b) then the prayer time expires;

c) the *excused* person still has ablution but renews it for no reason (*t*: i.e. not for the *excuse*);

d) then the *excuse* becomes active;

e) ablution is nullified.

The first ablution is not nullified by the expiration of the prayer time; it is nullified by the activation of the *excuse* after the new prayer time came in.

ABLUTION BEFORE THE PRAYER TIME

9.24 If an *excused* person makes ablution before the prayer time comes in and the *excuse* is active, that ablution is nullified by the expiration of that prayer time.

(*t*: For example, an *excused* person makes ablution for 'Asr (midafternoon) prayer just at the end of the Dhuhr (noon) prayer time.

a) The ablution is nullified with the expiration of the Dhuhr prayer time.

b) Ablution must be made in the 'Asr prayer time in order to pray the 'Asr prayer.)

FORESTALLING THE EXCUSE

9.25 If the *excused* person is capable of forestalling the *excuse*, as a non-virgin using a tampon to block istihada, then she is obliged to forestall it if there is no harm in doing so.

9.26 If the *excuse* is forestalled, then the *excused* status is cancelled.

WIPING FOOTGEAR (KHUFFAYN)

9.27 If the *excuse* is not active during ablution or while putting on footgear, then the *excused* person may wipe them for the legal duration.

9.28 The *excused* person may not wipe footgear, except during the prayer time one is in if:

a) footgear are put on while the *excuse* is active;

b) or footgear are put on after an ablution in which the *excuse* is active during that ablution.

THE PRAYER

9.29 If the *excuse* is activated by prostrating and is not active otherwise, then one prays by moving one's head while either standing or sitting.

An example is someone with a throat abscess that bleeds while prostrating and does not bleed while in an upright position.

9.30 If the *excuse* is activated while standing but not while sitting, then one prays sitting, just as the person who cannot read for the prayer for some reason while standing but can read while sitting.

9.31 An *excused* person may not lead the prayer of those who do not have chronic annulment of ablution.

9.32 It is permissible if both the imam (leader of the prayer) and the follower have the same *excuse*, or if the imam's *excuse* is lighter than the follower's *excuse*, such as the *excuse* of the imam is continually breaking wind and the *excuse* of the follower is urinary incontinence.

The follower's *excuse* is heavier because it is both the annulment of ritual purity and the existence of filth (najasa).

9.33 If the *excused* person makes ablution and while praying the prayer time expires, he must repeat the whole prayer after making another ablution.

He does not build on that prayer (i.e. start the prayer where he left off at the integral in which the prayer was invalidated) since the annulment of ablution by the *excuse* is real prior to the prayer time expiring.

9.34 If the *excuse* ceased before one makes ablution,

a) and while one is praying the prayer time expires;

b) and the *excuse* does not return until the prayer is completed;

then both the ablution and the prayer are valid.

CLEANING THE FILTH

9.35 If the amount of filth (najasa) is less than the size of a dirham (approximately 5 cm diameter), then it is overlooked in regard to the validity of the prayer.

9.36 If an amount of filth larger than the size of a dirham soils the clothes and/or body of the *excused* person, then cleaning it is obligatory if useful.

9.37 'Useful' means if during the time it takes to make ablution and pray the clothes and/or body would remain clean, then cleaning is obligatory.

9.38 In the case where the filth larger than the size of a dirham returns before an *excused* person has enough time to make ablution and pray, then washing the filth is not obligatory. The *excused* person prays in that state.

Part 2

The Commentary in Detail

قَال النَّبي ﷺ: « اللَّهُمَّ لا سَهْلَ إِلَّا ما جَعَلْتَهُ سَهْلاً،
وَأَنْتَ تَجْعَلُ الحَزْنَ إِذا شِئْتَ سَهْلاً »

The Prophet (Allah bless him and give him peace) said:

O *Allah*,
there is no ease except that which You make easy,
and You make the difficult,
if You will, easy.

10

Comprehensive Precepts

General Precepts

PRECEPT 1 It is obligatory for each woman to record her menstrual, lochial, and tuhr periods.

PRECEPT 2 Sexual intercourse is unlawful if the bleeding stops before the habit until the completion of the habit.

PRECEPT 3 Any colored discharge other than white takes the ruling of blood except for a woman in menopause.

PRECEPT 4 The color of the discharge is ascertained as soon as the kursuf is removed and the discharge is fresh; any change afterwards is disregarded.

PRECEPT 5 An incomplete tuhr is considered legal blood that links the first actual bleeding to the second actual bleeding.

PRECEPT 6 The habit changes with a valid blood or a valid tuhr.

PRECEPT 7 A complete but invalid tuhr separates between two bloods but cannot be used as the habit.

PRECEPT 8 The time it takes to take a purificatory bath (ghusl) is considered part of the menstrual or lochial period if it ends prior to the maximum.

Lochial Precepts

PRECEPT 9 There is no minimum for lochia.

PRECEPT 10 The maximum lochial period is 40 days (960 hours).

PRECEPT 11 It is obligatory to stop praying and fasting as soon as any bleeding occurs during the possible days of lochia.

PRECEPT 12 It is obligatory to take a purificatory bath (ghusl) if the bleeding stops any time within the possible days of lochia.

PRECEPT 13 The purificatory bath (ghusl) is obligatory if one reaches the lochial maximum and the bleeding continues.

PRECEPT 14 A mixed tuhr during the possible days of lochia is considered legal blood.

PRECEPT 15 If the blood does not exceed 40 days, all the blood is considered lochial provided there is a valid tuhr after it.

PRECEPT 16 If real or legal blood exceeds 40 days, she returns to her habit and all blood in excess of the habit is istihada.

PRECEPT 17 If real or legal blood exceeds 40 days, for someone with a habit, it is obligatory to make up the prayers missed in excess of the habit.

PRECEPT 18 Two lochial periods, or a lochial and a menstrual period, cannot succeed each other; there must be a complete tuhr between them.

PRECEPT 19 It is permissible to end lochia with actual tuhr that is considered legal blood.

PRECEPT 20 The purificatory bath (ghusl) is obligatory at the end of legal lochia.

PRECEPT 21 The minimal tuhr interval between two lochias is 6 months.

PRECEPT 22 The minimal tuhr interval between a lochial and menstrual period is 15 days (360 hours).

PRECEPT 23 Blood after a miscarried developed fetus is lochia.

Menstrual Precepts

PRECEPT 24 The minimal menstrual period is 3 days (72 hours).

PRECEPT 25 The maximum menstrual period is 10 days (240 hours).

PRECEPT 26 It is obligatory to stop praying and fasting as soon as any bleeding occurs after a complete tuhr, unless the bleeding occurs before the habit and if what remains of the tuhr-days added to the menstrual habit exceeds 10 days.

PRECEPT 27 Bleeding need not be constant to be menses. The first and last show of blood during the possible days of menstruation determine the legal ruling of menstruation, not the amount of blood during this time.

PRECEPT 28 Each time the blood stops before 3 days, she prays with ablution. Each time it stops after 3 days, she prays with a purificatory bath (ghusl).

PRECEPT 29 The purificatory bath (ghusl) is obligatory if one reaches the menstrual maximum and the bleeding continues.

PRECEPT 30 If real or legal blood stops before 3 days or after 10 days for someone with a habit, it is obligatory to make up the missed prayers.

PRECEPT 31 Two menstrual periods cannot succeed each other; there must be a complete tuhr interval between them.

PRECEPT 32 The minimal tuhr interval between two menstrual periods is 15 days (360 hours).

PRECEPT 33 A complete tuhr separates between two bloods. The blood before and after this tuhr are considered menstruation if they reach the minimum and there is nothing else prohibiting it.

PRECEPT 34 It is permissible for a woman with a habit to start and end a menstrual period with legal blood.

PRECEPT 35 The purificatory bath (ghusl) is obligatory at the end of legal menstruation.

PRECEPT 36 If the blood does not exceed 10 days, then all of it is menses provided there is a valid tuhr after it.

PRECEPT 37 If real or legal blood exceeds 10 days, and there is no minimum in the habitual place, then the place changes but the number remains the same from the onset of the blood; and the rest is istihada.

PRECEPT 38 If real or legal blood exceeds 10 days and a minimum occurs in the habitual place equal to the habit, then the habit remains the same and the rest is istihada.

PRECEPT 39 If real or legal blood exceeds 10 days and a minimum occurs in the habitual place but is less than the habit, then the number changes to the days that have occurred in the proper place and becomes the new habit, while the rest is istihada.

PRECEPT 40 A pregnant woman does not menstruate. Any bleeding during pregnancy is istihada.

PRECEPT 41 The blood before or after a miscarried embryo without discernible human features is menstruation if it reaches the minimum and comes after a complete tuhr.

11

Commentary on the Comprehensive Precepts

General Precepts

Precept 1

It is obligatory for each woman to record her menstrual, lochial, and tuhr periods.

11.1 The wisdom of this becomes clear when a problem appears and one must return to the habit i.e. the last valid blood and last valid tuhr. Normally, a woman's habit fluctuates. As long as the blood and/or tuhr fluctuate within the valid limits, there is no problem.

The problem starts when they are invalid. This usually happens unexpectedly. If a woman cannot remember her last valid habit or has not recorded it, then the problem gets complicated and serious since it concerns such matters as praying, fasting, etc.

We have provided some sample methods for recording menstruation, lochia, and tuhr in Appendix 2. However, you may record your habit any way you wish.

Precept 2

Sexual intercourse is unlawful if the bleeding stops before the habit until the completion of the habit.

11.2 This is because of the strong possibility of the blood returning according to its habit. However, she is required to pray and fast (dis: 14.1-20).

For example, a woman with a 7-day menstrual habit sees that her menses has stopped after day 5 of her habit.

a) She is obliged to take a bath (ghusl) and start to pray.

b) It is unlawful to have sexual intercourse on day 6 and day 7.

c) After the completion of the habit on day 7, sexual intercourse is permissible.

PRECEPT 3

Any colored discharge other than white takes the ruling of blood except for a woman in menopause.

11.3 For the non-menopausal woman, any colored discharge during the possible days of menstruation or lochia is considered menstruation or lochia unless it exceeds the maximum.

If the blood exceeds the maximum, then all the days over the habit are considered istihada (dysfunctional bleeding) and the missed prayers and fast-days must be made up.

11.4 The legal age of menopause is 55 lunar years (53 solar years and 4 months).

11.5 If a woman reaches the age of 55 and no longer has valid bleeding, then she is considered menopausal.

11.6 The color of menses for someone over 55 is either black or dark red; any other color is istihada.

a) However, if she has a colored discharge the same color she used to see during her menstruation before she reached 55, then it is menstruation.

b) If it is not the color she used to see, then it is istihada.

11.7 A woman who has menopause before she reaches the age of 55 does not legally classify as being menopausal.

1. If divorced, she must complete her postmarital waiting period ('idda) with 3 menstrual periods because there is no limit to tuhr.

2. If menstruation is brought on by medication to complete the postmarital waiting period, the blood is valid.

3. A hysterectomy entitles a woman, even if she has not reached 55, to complete her waiting period after a divorce by months.

PRECEPT 4

The color of the discharge is ascertained as soon as the kursuf is removed and the discharge is fresh; any change afterwards is disregarded.

11.8 The kursuf must have been placed properly (dis: 5.1) to determine the color of the discharge.

11.9 Discharge tends to oxidize when exposed to air. When that happens it generally changes color and becomes yellow.

1. If discharge is white when fresh and dries yellow, it is considered white.
2. If discharge is yellow when fresh and dries white, it is considered yellow.

PRECEPT 5

An incomplete tuhr is considered legal blood that links the first actual bleeding to the second actual bleeding.

11.10 If the tuhr is less than 15 days, whether it occurs during the place of the menstrual habit or not, it is considered legal blood.

1. The incomplete tuhr does not separate the two bloods and all of it is menstruation if the blood does not exceed the maximum.
2. If the blood exceeds the maximum, then that which is in excess of the maximum or the habit is istihada.

For example:

1. A menstrual beginner has 1 day of blood, then 14 days of tuhr, and then 1 day of blood.
    a) The tuhr is incomplete and joins the blood before and after it. These 16 days are legal blood.
    b) The first 10 days are menstruation.
2. Or a woman with a 10-day menstrual habit has 1 day of blood before her habit, then 10 days of tuhr, and then 1 day of blood.
    a) The tuhr is incomplete and joins the blood before and after it. These 12 days are legal blood.
    b) The 10 days of actual tuhr in her habitual place is menstruation.

c) The day before and after her habitual place is istihada (dysfunctional bleeding).

d) If her habit was less than 10 days, then she would return to her habit, and the excess is istihada.

PRECEPT 6

The habit changes with a valid blood or a valid tuhr.

11.11 The change could be in place or number or both.

11.12 The place of the habit changes if there is no blood in it.

For example, a woman has a 5-day menstrual habit and a 25-day tuhr habit.

1. She has 5-day menses, then 35-day tuhr and then 5-day menses.
2. The place of her menses moves from 25 days to 35 days.

11.13 The number of the habit changes if she has a valid blood or a valid tuhr different from the habit.

For example, a woman has a 5-day menstrual habit and a 25-day tuhr habit.

1. She has 3 days of menses in the habitual place, then 25 days of tuhr. This is a menstrual habit change from 5 days to 3 days.
2. Or, she has 5 days of menses, and then 23 days of tuhr. This is a tuhr habit change from 25 days to 23 days.

11.14 The number changes also if she has invalid blood that exceeds the maximum and at least the minimum amount occurs in the habitual place.

For example, a woman has a 5-day menstrual habit and a 25-day tuhr habit.

a) She has 5 days of menses, then 18 days of tuhr, then 11 days of blood.

b) The 11 days of blood are 7 days before its place and 4 days in its place.

c) The 11 days of blood are invalid because it exceeds the maximum.

d) The 4 days of blood occur in the habitual place, an amount over the minimal.

e) On day 5 of the habit, there is no blood.

f) She returns to her habit in terms of place, not number, because no blood occurs after day 5 to change it into legal blood.

g) The menstrual habit changes from 5 days to 4 days.

PRECEPT 7

A complete but invalid tuhr separates between two bloods but cannot be used as the habit.

11.15 A complete but invalid tuhr could come in various ways.

For example, after her 3-day menstrual period, a woman has 15 days of tuhr, then 1 day of blood, then 15 days of tuhr, and then 3 days of blood.

1. The first and last 3 days are menses because of the complete tuhr between them.
2. The 15 days of tuhr and the 1 day of istihada and the 15 days tuhr constitutes a 31-day invalid tuhr.
3. This 31-day invalid tuhr cannot be used as the habit.

PRECEPT 8

The time it takes to take a purificatory bath (ghusl) is considered part of the menstrual or lochial period if it ends prior to the maximum.

11.16 This is particularly important in Ramadan. If the menstrual or lochial period ends prior to the maximum before Fajr (Dawn) and the bath (ghusl) enters the time of Fajr, then she must imitate the fasting person this day, and then make up this fast-day.

11.17 This ruling also applies to the completion of the postmarital waiting period ('idda) and the right to revoke a one-fold or two-fold revocable divorce.

11.18 If one is unable to take a bath (ghusl) and qualifies to make tayammum (dry ablution), then the time the tayammum would take is considered part of the menstrual or lochial period (dis: 6.38-39).

Lochial Precepts

PRECEPT 9

There is no minimum for lochia.

11.19 If a woman sees no bleeding after giving birth, she is required to take a bath (ghusl) because there must be some blood, even if it is only on the baby.

11.20 If the bleeding stops immediately after birth, she is required to take a purificatory bath (ghusl) and pray.

PRECEPT 10

The maximum lochial period is 40 days (960 hours).

11.21 The maximum lochial period is 960 hours, 40 complete days. The time starts with the delivery of most of the baby (dis: 4.8-10).

PRECEPT 11

It is obligatory to stop praying and fasting as soon as any bleeding occurs during the possible days of lochia.

11.22 Until the 40 days are complete, any blood during the possible days of lochia is considered lochial (dis: Lochial Case One).

PRECEPT 12

It is obligatory to take a purificatory bath (ghusl) if the bleeding stops any time within the possible days of lochia.

11.23 There is a mistaken belief that a woman must wait the complete 40 days whether she is bleeding or not. This is incorrect as well as unlawful. Lochia comes to a legal end each time it stops during the possible days of lochia.

11.24 The bath (ghusl) is obligatory at the end of lochial bleeding.

11.25 When blood stops within the possible days of lochia, a bath (ghusl) becomes obligatory because there is no minimum.

However, when the blood stops before the minimum in menstruation, ablution, not a bath (ghusl), is required because the blood is istihada (dysfunctional bleeding).

PRECEPT 13

The purificatory bath (ghusl) is obligatory if one reaches the lochial maximum and the bleeding continues.

11.26 While there is bleeding during the possible days of lochia, one is obliged to wait until the maximum is reached; then the bath (ghusl) is obligatory even though there is bleeding.

11.27 For a lochial beginner, her habit will be the maximum.

For a woman with a habit, her habit remains and the blood over her habit is istihada. She must make up the missed prayers and fast-days.

PRECEPT 14

A mixed tuhr during the possible days of lochia is considered legal blood.

11.28 A mixed tuhr joins the blood before and after it. During the possible days of lochia, a show of blood after the birth and at the end of the 40 days is what determines the legal ruling of lochia for that duration, and not the amount of blood during this time. In other words, the blood does not have to be a constant flow.

11.29 A tuhr of 15 days or more during the possible days of lochia does not separate the blood before and after it; it joins them.

For example:

1. A lochial beginner gives birth, sees a spot of blood, then the bleeding stops, and then sees a spot of blood before the completion of day 40.
    a) The 40 days are lochia; from the time of the spot of blood she sees at the beginning until the spot of blood she sees at the end is lochia—even though there is no actual blood in between.
    b) Her lochial habit is 40 days.
2. If a lochial beginner gives birth and the blood stops on day 30 of the possible days of lochia, and then it returns after day 45.

a) Her lochial habit is 30 days.

b) In this case, the tuhr is complete and any blood after it would be considered menstruation if it reaches the minimum (72 hours); otherwise, it is istihada.

PRECEPT 15

If the blood does not exceed 40 days, all the blood is considered lochial provided there is a valid tuhr after it.

11.30 There must be a complete tuhr between lochial and menstrual blood.

For example, a woman has 35 days of lochia, then 15 days of tuhr, then on day 51 she sees blood, this would be menstruation if it completes the minimum (72 hours) (dis: Lochial Cases Three, Four and Five).

PRECEPT 16

If real or legal blood exceeds 40 days, she returns to her habit and all blood in excess of the habit is istihada.

11.31 As long as there is bleeding during the possible days of lochia, one is obliged to wait until the bleeding stops or the maximum is reached.

A record of the habit is needed to solve this situation (dis: Lochial Cases One and Two).

PRECEPT 17

If real or legal blood exceeds 40 days, for someone with a habit, it is obligatory to make up the prayers missed in excess of the habit.

11.32 As long as there is blood during the possible days of lochia one is obliged to wait (dis: Lochial Cases One and Two).

For example, the lochial habit is 20 days and the bleeding continues until day 41.

a) At the completion of day 40 even though there is bleeding, it is obligatory to take a bath (ghusl).

b) She must make up the prayers from day 21 to day 40.

PRECEPT 18

Two lochial periods, or a lochial and a menstrual period, cannot succeed each other; there must be a complete tuhr between them.

11.33 Any blood that exceeds the maximum cannot be lochial or menstrual; rather it is istihada because valid blood is not succeeded by valid blood.

11.34 A complete tuhr does not necessitate that it is a valid tuhr (dis: 11.15).

PRECEPT 19

It is permissible to end lochia with actual tuhr that is considered legal blood.

11.35 This is possible when real or legal blood exceeds the maximum (dis: Lochial Case One).

11.36 A lochial beginner is given a 40-day lochial habit if she has less than 40 days of blood, then an invalid tuhr, and then blood.

11.37 A woman with a lochial habit of 40 days, for example, who has a lochia of less than 40 days, then an invalid tuhr, and then blood, returns to her lochial habit (dis: Lochial Case Two).

PRECEPT 20

The purificatory bath (ghusl) is obligatory at the end of legal lochia.

11.38 A lochial beginner has less than 40 days of blood, then an invalid tuhr, and then blood. Even though the blood did not stop at day 40, in retrospect, she is given a 40-day lochial habit because of the invalid tuhr that follows it. In view of this, she is obliged to take a bath (ghusl) at the completion of day 40.

11.39 A woman with a lochial habit of 40 days who has a lochia of less than 40 days, for example, is advised to take a precautionary bath (ghusl) at the end of her habit (i.e. 40 days) in case something goes wrong.

11.40 If something goes wrong such as she happens to have an invalid tuhr after this blood of less than her habit, then she returns to her habit of 40 days, and the bath (ghusl) for the end of this legal lochia is obligatory.

11.41 If she did not take the bath (ghusl) at the end of her habit even though she did not see blood on day 40, then the prayers she performed after the habit are invalid and must be repeated.

(Dis: Lochial Cases One and Two.)

PRECEPT 21

The minimal tuhr interval between two lochias is 6 months.

11.42 The minimal tuhr between two lochias is set at 6 months because the minimal duration of pregnancy is 6 months.

However, with modern technology there are some rare cases of babies born with a gestation period of less than 6 months.

The duration of pregnancy relates to legal issues of paternity; see major works of jurisprudence for details.

11.43 If the tuhr interval between two lochias is less than 6 months, then the babies delivered are considered twins and the lochia starts with the birth of the former.

PRECEPT 22

The minimal tuhr interval between a lochial and menstrual period is 15 days (360 hours).

11.44 The minimal tuhr interval is 360 hours, 15 complete days.

11.45 Blood that appears after a tuhr less than 15 days is istihada (dysfunctional bleeding). She must continue to pray and fast even though there is bleeding.

PRECEPT 23

Blood after a miscarried developed fetus is lochia.

11.46 Legal pregnancy status is given if the miscarried fetus shows any human features like hair, hand, foot, finger, and/or fingernail.

1. The blood after a miscarried developed fetus is lochial and all the blood prior to the miscarriage is istihada.

2. All the other rulings related or dependant on birth and/or lochia are confirmed such as the end of the postmarital waiting period ('idda).

(Dis: 11.82-84 and Menstrual Case Fourteen for details of the miscarriage of an embryo.)

Menstrual Precepts

PRECEPT 24

The minimal menstrual period is 3 days (72 hours).

11.47 The minimal menstrual period is 72 hours, 3 complete days (dis: Precept 27, below).

11.48 During the possible days of menstruation a show of blood at the beginning and at the end is what determines the legal ruling of menses for that duration, and not the amount of blood during this time.

PRECEPT 25

The maximum menstrual period is 10 days (240 hours).

11.49 The maximum menstrual period is 240 hours, 10 complete days.

1. As long as there is bleeding during the possible days of menstruation, she is obliged to wait until the blood stops or she reaches the maximum.
2. As soon as the time reaches 240 hours, she is obliged to take a bath (ghusl).
3. If the bleeding exceeds the maximum, then she returns to her habit and all the bleeding over the habit is istihada.

For example, a woman has a 7-day menstrual habit and 20-day tuhr habit. After her 20-day tuhr, she has 11 days of blood.

1. Menstruation does not exceed 10 days.
2. When bleeding exceeds 10 days, it is certain that all of it cannot be menstruation.

3. She is obliged to take a bath (ghusl) although she is still bleeding as soon as she completes 240 hours.
4. In this case, she returns to her habit of 7 days, and day 8 to day 11 are istihada.
5. She is obliged to make up the prayers and fasts for these days of istihada.
6. Day 11 is definitely istihada, day 7 is certainly menstruation and the days between them are problematic.
7. A Sacred Law principle is that uncertainty does not remove certainty; thus, these questionable days are added to the istihada.

11.50 A menstrual beginner who reaches puberty with invalid or constant blood is given a menstrual habit of 10 days and a tuhr habit of 20.

PRECEPT 26

It is obligatory to stop praying and fasting as soon as any bleeding occurs after a complete tuhr, unless the bleeding occurs before the habit and if what remains of the tuhr-days added to the menstrual habit exceeds 10 days.

11.51 Every time a woman has blood after a complete tuhr she stops praying and fasting (dis: 3.50).

The exception to this is when the days prior to the habit are added to the habit and the total exceeds the maximum because of the strong probability that blood will appear in its habitual place.

For example, a woman has a 7-day menstrual habit and a 25-day tuhr habit.

a) She has her normal 7-day period, then 20 days of tuhr, and then blood.

b) She must continue her prayers for 5 more days to complete her tuhr habit of 25 days because if these 5 early days are added to the expected 7 habitual days, it would total 12 days.

11.52 Or if the early blood added to the habit does not exceed the maximum, she is required to stop praying.

For example, a woman has a 7-day menstrual habit and a 25-day tuhr habit.

a) She has her normal 7-day period, then 22 days of tuhr, and then blood.

b) She is required to stop praying because adding the 3 early days to the habit does not exceed the maximum.

c) If the blood stops before 3 days or exceeds 10 days, then she is obliged to make up the prayers of the days of istihada; those less than 3 days or those other than the habit.

11.53 Or as soon as she sees blood prior to her menstrual habit such that the remaining tuhr consists of a minimal menstruation and a valid tuhr, she is required to stop praying.

For example, a woman with a 3-day menstrual habit and a 40-day tuhr habit sees blood after 20 days of tuhr.

1. She is obliged to stop praying and fasting.
2. The blood she sees after day 20, if it reaches 3 days, is menses because it is preceded by a valid tuhr.
3. After these 3 days of menses there would be a valid tuhr of 17 days. Therefore, it separates the two bloods: the blood after day 20 and the blood after day 40.
4. The menstrual habit is applied if the blood exceeds 10 days, where it returns to the 3-day menstrual habit followed by a 17-day valid tuhr.

PRECEPT 27

Bleeding need not be constant to be menses. The first and last show of blood during the possible days of menstruation determine the legal ruling of menstruation, not the amount of blood during this time.

11.54 There is no stipulation that menstruation has to be a constant flow of blood. Heavy, light, frequent, or irregular bleeding is menstruation if it occurs during the possible days of menstruation.

For example:

1. A woman sees a spot of blood on Sunday morning at 7:00 A.M., then does not see anything until Wednesday morning at 6:45 A.M. at which time bleeding starts, and ends at 7:05 A.M.
2. Or she has a constant flow from Sunday morning to Wednesday morning.

Each case above is menstruation. In the first case, the time between the two spots of blood is legal blood and invalidates the prayer and fast.

In either case, if the bleeding ceases just before 7:00 A.M. on Wednesday and there is no bleeding for the next 15 days, the bleeding is istihada (dysfunctional bleeding), not menses.

PRECEPT 28

Each time the blood stops before 3 days, she prays with ablution. Each time it stops after 3 days, she prays with a purificatory bath (ghusl).

11.55 If the blood stops any time before the minimum during the possible days of menstruation, then she is obliged to wait until the end of the preferred prayer time, make ablution, and pray if the blood does not return.

1. During Ramadan, she must fast if the blood stops at night or imitate the one who fasts if the blood stops during the day because of the sacredness of the month.
2. If the blood returns during the possible days of menstruation, her tuhr status is cancelled and she must stop praying and fasting.
3. If the blood stops any time after the minimum during the possible days of menstruation but before the habit, then she is obliged to wait until the end of the preferred prayer time, take a bath (ghusl), and pray.

11.56 If the blood exceeds the habit during the possible days of menstruation, she must either wait for it to stop or for the completion of 10 days.

Postponing the bath (ghusl) to the end of the preferred prayer time is recommended but not obligatory because the return of blood after the habit is unlikely.

11.57 She prays with ablution if the blood stops before the minimum because it is istihada.

11.58 Every time the blood stops after the minimum, she takes a bath (ghusl) and prays because the blood is menses.

PRECEPT 29

The purificatory bath (ghusl) is obligatory if one reaches the menstrual maximum and the bleeding continues.

11.59 As long as there is bleeding during the possible days of menstruation, one is obliged to wait. Once the maximum is reached, then the bath (ghusl) is obligatory even though there is bleeding.

11.60 For a menstrual beginner, her habit is the maximum (10 days).

For a woman with a habit, her habit remains and the blood over her habit is istihada. She must make up the missed prayers and fast-days.

PRECEPT 30

If real or legal blood stops before 3 days or after 10 days for someone with a habit, it is obligatory to make up the missed prayers.

11.61 If a woman sees blood during the possible days of menstruation, she is obliged to stop praying and fasting.

1. Blood less than the minimum is istihada.
2. Blood over the maximum is istihada.
3. Blood over the habit when it exceeds the maximum is istihada.

11.62 The invalidity of this blood is realized in retrospect. Because of this, she must make up the missed prayers and fast-days, though there is no sin for having missed them.

PRECEPT 31

Two menstrual periods cannot succeed each other; there must be a complete tuhr interval between them.

11.63 Any blood that exceeds the maximum cannot be menstrual, rather it is istihada because valid blood is not succeeded by valid blood.

11.64 A complete tuhr does not necessitate that it be a valid tuhr.

PRECEPT 32

The minimal tuhr interval between two menstrual periods is 15 days (360 hours).

11.65 The minimal tuhr interval is 360 hours, 15 complete days.

11.66 Some people mistakenly suppose that if a woman has bleeding *before* the 15-day minimum, as soon as she reaches day 15 she stops praying and fasting. They incorrectly assume that the blood after day 15 is menses.

11.67 Unless her tuhr habit is 15 days, she is obliged to continue praying and fasting until she completes the days of her tuhr habit (dis: Menstrual Cases Fifteen and Sixteen).

For example, if she has a 20-day tuhr habit, she must continue praying and fasting until she completes her habit of 20 days.

If the bleeding continues (i.e. completes the tuhr habit and continues into the place of the menstrual habit), then and only then does she stop praying and fasting.

PRECEPT 33

A complete tuhr separates two bloods. The blood before and after this tuhr are considered menstruation if they reach the minimum and there is nothing else prohibiting it.

11.68 'Nothing else prohibiting it' means that the blood does not occur during pregnancy, nor is it caused by an illness.

11.69 If a complete tuhr occurs between two bloods, it separates them.

1. The blood before and after the tuhr are menstruation if each of them reach or exceed the minimum as long as there is nothing prohibiting it, such as pregnancy.
2. If one of them does not reach the minimum or there is something prohibiting it, then the blood is either istihada or lochia.

   For example, a woman bleeds during pregnancy for 5 days, then has a 15-day tuhr interval, and then gives birth.

   The second blood is lochial and the first blood is istihada, even though there is a complete tuhr in between them.

Note, a tuhr could be complete but invalid at the same time (dis: Precept 7).

PRECEPT 34

It is permissible for a woman with a habit to start and end a menstrual period with legal blood.

11.70 It is permissible to start and end a menstrual period with actual tuhr only if there is blood before and after it.

For example, a woman with a 10-day menstrual habit has 1 day of blood before her habit place, then 14 days of tuhr, and then 1 day of blood.

The 10 days of actual tuhr that fit in the habitual place are menstruation.

This is how a menstrual period might begin and end with legal, not actual blood.

11.71 It is permissible for the menstrual beginner to end the menstrual period with actual tuhr only if there is blood after it.

For example, a menstrual beginner has 1 day of blood, then 14 days of tuhr, and then 1 day of blood. The 14-day tuhr is incomplete and occurs between two bloods but does not legally separate them.

The first 10 days are menstruation.

This is how a menstrual period might end with legal and not actual blood (dis: Menstrual Case Five).

PRECEPT 35

The purificatory bath (ghusl) is obligatory at the end of legal menstruation.

11.72 A woman must take a bath (ghusl) when ending a legal menstrual period even though there is no blood. This is precautionary when everything is normal.

11.73 This bath (ghusl) becomes obligatory when there are some irregularities in the cycle and the habit must be stamped to correct the invalid bleeding and/or invalid tuhr (dis: Menstrual Case Five).

For example, if a menstrual beginner has 1 day of blood, then 14 days of tuhr, and then 1 day of blood, the 14-day tuhr is incomplete and joins the blood that comes before and after it.

1. The first 10 days are menstruation.

2. Puberty is confirmed in retrospect from the first day.
3. She must take a bath (ghusl) at the end of day 10 from the beginning of blood on the first day, even though there in no actual bleeding at this time.
4. She is also obliged to make up these 10 fast-days if Ramadan.
5. She is required to know these rulings prior to their occurrence because knowledge of the 'personally obligatory religious knowledge' is personally obligatory.
6. If she does not know these rulings, she must ask a scholar immediately.
7. If she did not take a bath (ghusl) after 240 hours from the first sighting of blood (i.e. at the end of legal menstruation), then the prayers of day 11, day 12, day 13, and day 14 are invalid and she must make them up. However, the fasts are valid.

PRECEPT 36

If the blood does not exceed 10 days, then all of it is menses provided there is a valid tuhr after it.

11.74 It is not unusual for menstruation to fluctuate. There is no problem as long as it is within the valid limits (dis: Menstrual Cases Six to Eleven).

11.75 If the tuhr is invalid, then all the days in excess of the habit are istihada (dysfunctional bleeding) and the missed prayers must be made up.

The habit does not change and should thus be noted in the record.

PRECEPT 37

If real or legal blood exceeds 10 days and there is no minimum in the habitual place, then the place changes but the number remains the same from the onset of the blood, and the rest is istihada.

11.76 The record of the habit is needed to solve this problem (dis: Menstrual Cases One and Two).

PRECEPT 38

If real or legal blood exceeds 10 days and a minimum occurs in the habitual place equal to the habit, then the habit remains the same and the rest is istihada.

11.77 Istihada could be blood before and/or after the habitual menstruation.

The record of the habit is needed to solve this problem (dis: Menstrual Cases Four and Five).

PRECEPT 39

If real or legal blood exceeds 10 days and a minimum occurs in the habitual place but is less than the habit, then the number changes to the days that have occurred in the proper place and becomes the new habit, while the rest is istihada.

11.78 The record of the habit is needed to solve this problem (dis: Menstrual Case Six).

PRECEPT 40

A pregnant woman does not menstruate. Any bleeding during pregnancy is istihada.

11.79 Bleeding during pregnancy is istihada (dysfunctional bleeding) even if it occurs in the place of the habit.

11.80 The lining of the uterus, which makes up the menstrual blood, does not shed during pregnancy.

11.81 Any blood during pregnancy must be recorded.

PRECEPT 41

The blood before or after a miscarried embryo without discernible human features is menstruation if it reaches the minimum and comes after a complete tuhr.

11.82 Any blood during pregnancy must be recorded. The record of the habit is needed to solve this problem.

11.83 A woman's legal status of pregnancy is canceled with a miscarriage of an embryo. Any blood that occurred during the time she was pregnant takes the ruling of legal menstruation if it fits in its habit.

The blood after the pregnancy ended with a miscarried embryo is not lochia; it is menstruation or istihada, according to the habit (dis: Menstrual Case Fourteen).

For the miscarriage of a developed fetus see 11.46.

12

Lochial Case Studies

1. Exceed the Maximum

    Case One: 10 days blood – 20 days tuhr – 11 days blood

    Case Two: 1 day blood – 30 days tuhr – 1 day blood – 14 days tuhr – 1 day blood

2. Do Not Exceed the Maximum

    Case Three: 5 days blood – 34 days tuhr – 1 day blood

    Case Four: 18 days blood – 22 days tuhr – 1 day blood

    Case Five: 1 day blood – 34 days tuhr – 1 day blood – 15 days tuhr – 1 day blood

Lochial Case Studies

Case One

SITUATION: A woman has a 20-day lochial habit. She gives birth and has 10 days of blood, then 20 days of tuhr, and then 11 days of blood.

HABIT

1	-	-	-	-	-	-	-	-	10	11	-	-	-	-	-	-	-	-	20
20 lochia																			

SITUATION

1	-	-	-	-	-	-	-	-	10	11	-	-	-	-	-	-	-	-	20	21	-	-	-	-	-	-	-	-	30	31	-	-	-	-	-	-	-	-	40	41
10 blood										20 tuhr																				11 blood										

1. *Analysis of the Situation*
    1. The blood from day 1 to day 10 is lochia given that it came after childbirth.
    2. The tuhr from day 11 to day 30 is a mixed tuhr, complete in terms of length, invalid because it occurs during the possible days of lochia. This tuhr is legal blood, and it is added to the blood before and after it.
    3. The blood from day 31 to day 41 is added to all the previous blood: 10 days of actual blood and 20 days of legal blood.
    4. Total blood equals 41 days.

2. *Solution*
    1. Since the bleeding exceeds 40 days, she returns to her lochial habit.
    2. The first 20 days after giving birth is legal lochia: from day 1 to day 10 of actual blood and day 11 to day 20 of legal blood.
    3. Then 21 days is istihada: from day 21 to day 30 of actual tuhr and day 31 to day 41 of legal tuhr.

SOLUTION

1	-	-	-	-	-	-	-	-	10	11	-	-	-	-	-	-	-	-	20	21	-	-	-	-	-	-	-	-	30	31	-	-	-	-	-	-	-	-	40	41
20 lochia																				21 istihada																				

3. *Rulings for the Day-by-Day Situation*

1. Lochia begins after giving birth; it is unlawful to pray or fast.
2. When the blood stops on day 11, she is required to take a purificatory bath (ghusl), pray, and fast if Ramadan.
3. Sexual intercourse is unlawful from day 11 to day 20 even though she is not bleeding because of the likelihood of the blood returning during its habitual time. However, she is required to pray and fast.
4. It is precautionary that she take a bath (ghusl) at the end of her habit on day 20, even though she does not see blood, because of the possibility of returning to her habit.
5. With the return of blood on day 31, she must stop praying and fasting.
6. The blood on day 31 invalidates the previous tuhr from day 11 to day 30 because it is a mixed tuhr.
7. With the completion of day 40, she must take a bath (ghusl) whether the bleeding stops or not.
8. The blood on day 41 makes clear that the bleeding exceeds the maximum and the day-by-day rulings for this situation need to be revised (see below).

4. *Revision of the Day-by-Day Rulings*

1. Since the bleeding exceeds 40 days, she returns to her lochial habit.
2. Day 11 to day 20:

   The ruling of tuhr is canceled and based on this:

   a) Prayers are invalid because she prayed while in legal lochia, though there is no sin for having done so. She need not repeat the prayers unless they were make-up prayers or a vowed prayer; then she must repeat them.
   b) If she fasted an obligatory or wajib fast, she must make them up, though there is no sin upon her for having fasted.
3. Day 21 to day 30:
   1) Her fasts are valid.
   2) The validity of her prayers depends on the following:

    a) If she took a precautionary bath (ghusl) on day 20, then her prayers are valid.
    b) If she did not take a precautionary bath (ghusl), then the prayers are invalid and must be repeated.

4. Day 31 to day 40:

   The ruling of lochia is canceled and based on this:

    a) She must make up the prayers omitted, though there is no sin for not having prayed them.
    b) She must make up the fast-days if in Ramadan, though there is no sin for not having fasted these days.

5. *Precepts Applied for This Situation*

1. It is obligatory for each woman to record her menstrual, lochial, and tuhr periods.
2. It is obligatory to stop praying and fasting as soon as any bleeding occurs during the possible days of lochia.
3. It is obligatory to take a purificatory bath (ghusl) if the bleeding stops any time within the possible days of lochia.
4. Sexual intercourse is unlawful if the bleeding stops before the habit until the completion of the habit.
5. A mixed tuhr during the possible days of lochia is considered legal blood.
6. It is permissible to end lochia with actual tuhr that is considered legal blood.
7. The purificatory bath (ghusl) is obligatory at the end of legal lochia.
8. If real or legal blood exceeds 40 days, she returns to her habit and all blood in excess of the habit is istihada.
9. If real or legal blood exceeds 40 days, for someone with a habit, it is obligatory to make up the prayers missed in excess of the habit.

Notes

Case Two

SITUATION: A woman has a 20-day lochial habit. She gives birth and has 1 day of blood, then 30 days of tuhr, then 1 day of blood, then 14 days of tuhr, and then 1 day of blood.

HABIT

<table>
<tr><td>1</td><td>2</td><td>-</td><td>-</td><td>-</td><td>-</td><td>-</td><td>-</td><td>-</td><td>-</td><td>-</td><td>-</td><td>-</td><td>-</td><td>-</td><td>-</td><td>-</td><td>-</td><td>20</td></tr>
<tr><td colspan="19">20 lochia</td></tr>
</table>

SITUATION

<table>
<tr><td>1</td><td>2</td><td>-</td><td>-</td><td>-</td><td>-</td><td>-</td><td>-</td><td>-</td><td>-</td><td>-</td><td>-</td><td>-</td><td>-</td><td>-</td><td>-</td><td>-</td><td>-</td><td>20</td><td>21</td><td>-</td><td>-</td><td>-</td><td>-</td><td>31</td><td>32</td><td>33</td><td>-</td><td>-</td><td>-</td><td>-</td><td>-</td><td>40</td><td>-</td><td>-</td><td>-</td><td>-</td><td>-</td><td>46</td><td>47</td></tr>
<tr><td>b</td><td colspan="24">30 tuhr</td><td>b</td><td colspan="13">14 tuhr</td><td>b</td></tr>
</table>

1. *Analysis of the Situation*

    1. The blood on day 1 is lochia given that it came after childbirth.
    2. The tuhr from day 2 to day 31 is a mixed tuhr, complete in terms of length, invalid because it occurs during the possible days of lochia. This tuhr is legal blood, and it is added to the blood before and after it.
    3. The blood on day 32 is added to all the previous blood: the 1 day of actual blood and the 30 days of legal blood.
    4. The tuhr from day 33 to day 46 is an invalid tuhr because it is less than 15 days and does not separate between day 32 and day 47. This tuhr is legal blood, and it is added to the blood before and after it.
    5. The blood on day 47 is added to all the previous real and legal blood.
    6. Total blood equals 47 days.

2. *Solution*

    1. Since the bleeding exceeds 40 days, she returns to her lochial habit.
    2. The first 20 days after giving birth is legal lochia: from day 1 of actual blood and day 2 to day 20 of legal blood.
    3. Then 27 days is istihada: from day 21 to day 31 of actual tuhr, then day 32 of legal tuhr, then from day 33 to day 46 of actual tuhr, and day 47 of legal tuhr.

SOLUTION

<table>
<tr><td>1</td><td>2</td><td>-</td><td>-</td><td>-</td><td>-</td><td>-</td><td>-</td><td>-</td><td>-</td><td>-</td><td>-</td><td>-</td><td>-</td><td>-</td><td>-</td><td>-</td><td>-</td><td>20</td><td>21</td><td>-</td><td>-</td><td>-</td><td>-</td><td>31</td><td>32</td><td>33</td><td>-</td><td>-</td><td>-</td><td>-</td><td>-</td><td>40</td><td>-</td><td>-</td><td>-</td><td>-</td><td>-</td><td>46</td><td>47</td></tr>
<tr><td colspan="19">20 lochia</td><td colspan="21">27 istihada</td></tr>
</table>

3. *Rulings for the Day-by-Day Situation*

1. Lochia begins after giving birth; it is unlawful to pray or fast.
2. When the blood stops on day 2, she is required to take a purificatory bath (ghusl), pray, and fast if Ramadan.
3. Sexual intercourse is unlawful from day 2 to day 20 even though she is not bleeding because of the likelihood of the blood returning during its habitual time. However, she is required to pray and fast.
4. It is precautionary that she take a bath (ghusl) at the end of her habit on day 20, even though she does not see blood because of the possibility of returning to her habit.
5. With the return of blood on day 32, she must stop praying and fasting.
6. The blood on day 32 invalidates the previous tuhr from day 2 to day 31 because it is a mixed tuhr.
7. When the blood stops on day 33, she is required to take a bath (ghusl), pray, and fast.
8. The blood on day 47 makes clear that the previous tuhr is incomplete and joins between day 32 and day 47. Thus, the bleeding exceeds the maximum and the day-by-day rulings for this situation need to be revised.
9. She must pray and fast on day 47; the blood is istihada because it follows an incomplete tuhr.

4. *Revision of the Day-by-Day Rulings*

1. Since the bleeding exceeds 40 days, she returns to her lochial habit.
2. Day 2 to day 20:

   The ruling of tuhr is canceled and based on this:

   a) Prayers are invalid because she prayed while in legal lochia, though there is no sin for having done so. She need not repeat the prayers unless they were make-up prayers or a vowed prayer; then she must repeat them.
   b) If she fasted an obligatory or wajib fast, then she must make them up; however, there is no sin upon her for having fasted.

3. Day 21 to day 31:
    1) Her fasts are valid.
    2) The validity of the prayers depends on the following:
        a) If she took a bath (ghusl) on day 20, then her prayers are valid.
        b) If she did not take a bath (ghusl), then the prayers are invalid and must be repeated.
4. Day 32:

    The ruling of lochia is canceled and based on this:
    a) She must make up the prayers she omitted, though there is no sin for not having prayed them.
    b) She must make up the fast-day if in Ramadan, though there is no sin for not having fasted.
5. Day 33 to 47:

    The prayers and fasts are valid.

5. *Precepts Applied for This Situation*

1. It is obligatory for each woman to record her menstrual, lochial, and tuhr periods.
2. It is obligatory to stop praying and fasting as soon as any bleeding occurs during the possible days of lochia.
3. It is obligatory to take a purificatory bath (ghusl) if the bleeding stops any time within the possible days of lochia.
4. Sexual intercourse is unlawful if the bleeding stops before the habit until the completion of the habit.
5. A mixed tuhr during the possible days of lochia is considered legal blood.
6. An incomplete tuhr is considered legal blood that links the first actual bleeding to the second actual bleeding.
7. It is permissible to end lochia with actual tuhr that is considered legal blood.
8. The purificatory bath (ghusl) is obligatory at the end of legal lochia.
9. If real or legal blood exceeds 40 days, she returns to her habit and all blood in excess of the habit is istihada.
10. If real or legal blood exceeds 40 days, for someone with a habit, it is obligatory to make up the prayers missed in excess of the habit.

Notes

Lochial Case Two

Case Three

SITUATION: A woman has a 20-day lochial habit. She gives birth and has 5 days of blood, then 34 days of tuhr, and then 1 day of blood.

HABIT

1	-	-	-	-	-	-	-	-	10	11	-	-	-	-	-	-	-	-	20
20 lochia																			

SITUATION

1	-	-	-	5	6	-	-	-	-	-	-	-	-	-	-	-	-	-	20	21	-	-	-	-	-	-	-	-	-	-	-	-	-	-	-	-	-	39	40
5 blood					34 tuhr																																		b

1. *Analysis of the Situation*
    1. The blood from day 1 to day 5 is lochia given that it came after childbirth.
    2. The tuhr from day 6 to day 39 is a mixed tuhr, complete in terms of length, invalid because it occurs during the possible days of lochia. This tuhr is legal blood, and it is added to the blood before and after it.
    3. The blood on day 40 is added to all the previous blood: the 5 days of actual blood and the 34 days of legal blood.
    4. Total blood equals 40 days.

2. *Solution*

    There is a new lochial habit of 40 days if followed by a valid tuhr.

SOLUTION

1	-	-	-	5	6	-	-	-	-	-	-	-	-	-	-	-	-	-	20	21	-	-	-	-	-	-	-	-	-	-	-	-	-	-	-	-	-	39	40
40 lochia																																							

3. *Rulings for the Day-by-Day Situation*
    1. Lochia begins after giving birth; it is unlawful to pray or fast.

2. When the blood stops on day 6, she is required to take a purificatory bath (ghusl), pray, and fast if Ramadan.
3. Sexual intercourse is unlawful from day 6 to day 20 even though she is not bleeding because of the likelihood of the blood returning during its habitual time. However, she is required to pray and fast.
4. It is precautionary that she take a bath (ghusl) at the end of her habit on day 20, even though she does not see blood, because of the possibility of returning to her habit.
5. With the return of blood on day 40, she must stop praying and fasting.
6. The blood on day 40 invalidates the previous tuhr from day 6 to day 39 because it is a mixed tuhr, and the day-by-day rulings for this situation need to be revised.
7. When the bleeding stops on day 40, she is required to take a bath (ghusl), pray, and fast.

4. *Revision of the Day-by-Day Rulings*

1. The lochial habit changes to 40 days.
2. Day 6 to day 39:

   The ruling of tuhr is canceled and based on this:

   a) Prayers are invalid because she prayed while in legal lochia, though there is no sin for having done so. She need not repeat the prayers unless they were make-up prayers or a vowed prayer; then she must repeat them.
   b) If she fasted an obligatory or wajib fast, then she must make them up, though there is no sin upon her for having fasted.

5. *Precepts Applied for This Situation*

1. It is obligatory for each woman to record her menstrual, lochial, and tuhr periods.
2. It is obligatory to stop praying and fasting as soon as any bleeding occurs during the possible days of lochia.
3. It is obligatory to take a purificatory bath (ghusl) if the bleeding stops any time within the possible days of lochia.
4. Sexual intercourse is unlawful if the bleeding stops before the habit until the completion of the habit.
5. A mixed tuhr during the possible days of lochia is considered legal blood.
6. If the blood does not exceed 40 days, then all the blood is considered lochial provided there is a valid tuhr after it.
7. The habit changes with a valid blood or a valid tuhr.

Notes

Case Four

SITUATION: A woman has a 20-day lochial habit. She gives birth and has 18 days of blood, then 22 days of tuhr, and then 1 day of blood.

HABIT

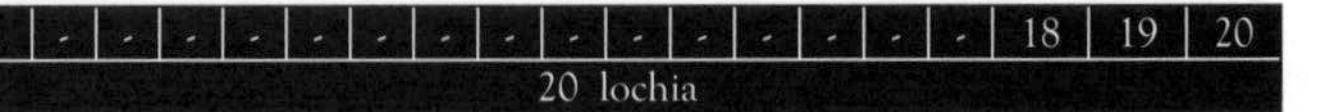

SITUATION

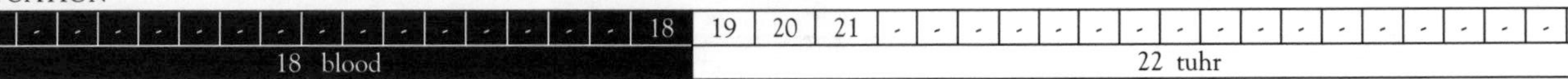

1. *Analysis of the Situation*

    1. The blood on day 1 to day 18 is lochia given that it came after childbirth.
    2. The tuhr from day 19 to day 40 is valid because the second blood occurs after the possible days of lochia.
    3. The blood on day 41 is istihada because it occurs after the possible days of lochia and is less than the minimal menstruation period. If the bleeding were to reach the minimum, then it would be menstruation.

2. *Solution*

    1. There is a new lochia habit of 18 days because there is a valid tuhr interval after it.
    2. Day 1 to day 18 is lochia.
    3. Day 19 to day 40 is tuhr.
    4. Day 41 is istihada.

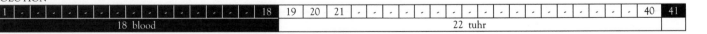

SOLUTION

1 - - - - - - - - - - - - - - - 18 19 20 21 - - - - - - - - - - - - - - - - - - 40 41

18 blood

22 tuhr

3. *Rulings for the Day-by-Day Situation*

1. Lochia begins after giving birth; it is unlawful to pray or fast.
2. When the blood stops on day 19, she is required to take a purificatory bath (ghusl), pray, and fast if Ramadan.
3. Sexual intercourse is unlawful from day 19 to day 20 even though she is not bleeding because of the likelihood of the blood returning during its habitual time. However, she is required to pray and fast.
4. It is precautionary that she take a bath (ghusl) at the end of her habit on day 20, even though she does not see blood because of the possibility of returning to her habit.
5. At the end of day 40, it becomes clear that the tuhr from day 19 to day 40 is a complete valid tuhr that separates between the blood before and after it. Thus, the lochia habit changes to 18 days.
6. With the return of blood on day 41, she must stop praying and fasting because it occurs after a valid tuhr.
7. When the bleeding stops on day 41 before the minimum, it is clear that it is istihada.
    a) She must make up the prayers she omitted, though there is no sin for not having prayed them.
    b) She must make up the fast-day if in Ramadan, though there is no sin for having not fasted this day.

4. *Precepts Applied for This Situation*

1. It is obligatory for each woman to record her menstrual, lochial, and tuhr periods.
2. It is obligatory to stop praying and fasting as soon as any bleeding occurs during the possible days of lochia.
3. It is obligatory to take a purificatory bath (ghusl) if the bleeding stops any time within the possible days of lochia.
4. Sexual intercourse is unlawful if the bleeding stops before the habit until the completion of the habit.
5. If the blood does not exceed 40 days, then all the blood is considered lochial provided there is a valid tuhr after it.
6. The habit changes with a valid blood or a valid tuhr.
7. If real or legal blood stops before 3 days or after 10 days, for someone with a habit, it is obligatory to make up the missed prayers.

Case Five

SITUATION: A woman has a 20-day lochial habit. She gives birth and has 1 day of blood, then 34 days of tuhr, then 1 day of blood, then 15 days of tuhr, and then 1 day of blood.

HABIT

<table>
<tr><td>1</td><td>-</td><td>-</td><td>-</td><td>-</td><td>-</td><td>-</td><td>-</td><td>-</td><td>10</td><td>11</td><td>-</td><td>-</td><td>-</td><td>-</td><td>-</td><td>-</td><td>-</td><td>-</td><td>20</td></tr>
<tr><td colspan="20">20 lochia</td></tr>
</table>

SITUATION

<table>
<tr><td>1</td><td>2</td><td>-</td><td>-</td><td>-</td><td>-</td><td>-</td><td>-</td><td>-</td><td>-</td><td>-</td><td>-</td><td>-</td><td>20</td><td>21</td><td>-</td><td>-</td><td>-</td><td>-</td><td>-</td><td>-</td><td>-</td><td>-</td><td>-</td><td>35</td><td>36</td><td>37</td><td>-</td><td>-</td><td>40</td><td>-</td><td>-</td><td>-</td><td>-</td><td>-</td><td>-</td><td>-</td><td>-</td><td>51</td><td>52</td></tr>
<tr><td>b</td><td colspan="24">34 tuhr</td><td>b</td><td colspan="13">15 tuhr</td><td>b</td></tr>
</table>

1. *Analysis of the Situation*
    1. The blood on day 1 is lochia given that it came after childbirth.
    2. The tuhr from day 2 to day 35 is a mixed tuhr, complete in terms of length, invalid because it occurs during the possible days of lochia. This tuhr is legal blood, and it is added to the blood before and after it.
    3. The blood on day 36 is added to all the previous blood: the 1 day of actual blood and the 34 days of legal blood.
    4. The tuhr from day 37 to day 51 is a valid tuhr because it is 15 days, and it separates between day 36 and day 52. The blood of day 52 occurs after the possible days of lochia.
    5. The blood on day 52 is istihada. If the bleeding were to reach the minimum, then it would be menstruation.
    6. Total days of continuous blood equal 36 days.
2. *Solution*
    1. There is a new lochia habit of 36 days because there is a valid tuhr interval after it.
    2. Day 1 to day 36 is lochia.
    3. Day 37 to day 51 is tuhr.
    4. Day 52 is istihada.

SOLUTION

1	2	-	-	-	-	-	-	-	-	-	-	-	20	21	-	-	-	-	-	-	-	-	-	35	36	37	-	-	40	-	-	-	-	-	-	-	-	51	52
36 lochia																										15 tuhr													

3. *Rulings for the Day-by-Day Situation*

1. Lochia begins after giving birth; it is unlawful to pray or fast.
2. When the blood stops on day 2, she is required to take a purificatory bath (ghusl), pray, and fast if Ramadan.
3. Sexual intercourse is unlawful from day 2 to day 20 even though she is not bleeding because of the likelihood of the blood returning during its habitual time. However, she is required to pray and fast.
4. It is precautionary that she take a bath (ghusl) at the end of her habit on day 20, even though she does not see blood, because of the possibility of returning to her habit.
5. With the return of blood on day 36, she must stop praying and fasting.
6. The blood on day 36 invalidates the previous tuhr from day 2 to day 35 because it is a mixed tuhr.
7. When the blood stops on day 37, she must take a bath (ghusl), pray, and fast.
8. At the end of day 51, it becomes clear that the tuhr from day 37 to day 51 is a valid tuhr that separates between the blood before and after it. Thus, the habit changes to 36 days and the day-by-day rulings for this situation need to be revised.
9. With the return of blood on day 52, she must stop praying and fasting because it occurs after a valid tuhr and it could be menstruation if the bleeding reaches the minimum.

4. *Revision of the Day-by-Day Rulings*

1. The lochial habit changes to 36 days because there is a valid tuhr after it.
2. Day 2 to day 35:

   The ruling of tuhr is canceled and based on this:

   a) Prayers are invalid because she prayed while in legal lochia, though there is no sin for having done so. She need not repeat the prayers unless they were make-up prayers or a vowed prayer; then she must repeat them.

    b) If she fasted an obligatory or wajib fast, then she must make them up; however, there is no sin upon her for having fasted.

3. Day 37 to day 51:

   Her prayers and fast-days are valid.

4. Day 52:

   With the cessation of bleeding before the minimum, it is clear that this blood is istihada.

    a) She must make up the prayers omitted, though there is no sin for not having prayed them.
    b) She must make up the fast-day if in Ramadan, though there is no sin for not having fasted this day.

5. *Precepts Applied for This Situation*

1. It is obligatory for each woman to record her menstrual, lochial, and tuhr periods.
2. It is obligatory to stop praying and fasting as soon as any bleeding occurs during the possible days of lochia.
3. It is obligatory to take a purificatory bath (ghusl) if the bleeding stops any time within the possible days of lochia.
4. Sexual intercourse is unlawful if the bleeding stops before the habit until the completion of the habit.
5. A mixed tuhr during the possible days of lochia is considered legal blood.
6. If the blood does not exceed the maximum, then all the blood is considered lochia provided there is a valid tuhr after it.
7. The habit changes with a valid blood or a valid tuhr.
8. If real or legal blood stops before 3 days or after 10 days, for someone with a habit, it is obligatory to make up the missed prayers.

Notes

13

Menstrual Case Studies

1. Less than minimum in the habitual place

    Case One: 5 days blood – 15 days tuhr – 11 days blood

    Case Two: 5 days blood – 64 days tuhr – 11 days blood

    Case Three: 5 days blood – 46 days tuhr – 11 days blood

2. Minimal amount in the habitual place equal to the habit

    Case Four: 5 days blood – 48 days tuhr – 12 days blood

    Case Five: 5 days blood – 54 days tuhr – 1 day blood – 14 days tuhr – 1 day blood

3. Minimal amount not equal to the habit in the habitual place

    Case Six: 5 days blood – 57 days tuhr – 3 days blood – 14 days tuhr – 1 day blood

4. Not exceeding the maximum

    Case Seven: 5 days blood - 55 days tuhr - 9 days blood

    Case Eight: 5 days blood - 50 days tuhr - 10 days blood

    Case Nine: 5 days blood - 54 days tuhr - 8 days blood

    Case Ten: 5 days blood - 50 days tuhr - 7 days blood

    Case Eleven: 5 days blood - 58 days tuhr - 3 days blood

    Case Twelve: 5 days blood - 64 days tuhr - 7 days blood

5. Lochia succeeded by menstrual period

    Case Thirteen: 1 day blood - 25 days tuhr - 1 day blood - 14 days tuhr - 1 day

6. Miscarried embryo

    Case Fourteen: 7 days blood - 30 days tuhr - 15 days blood - miscarriage

7. Incomplete tuhr

    Case Fifteen: 5 days blood - 14 days tuhr - 5 days blood

    Case Sixteen: 5 days blood - 14 days tuhr - 9 days blood

Case One

SITUATION: A woman has a 5-day menstrual habit and a 55-day tuhr habit. She has her usual 5 days of menstruation, then 15 days of tuhr, and then 11 days of blood.

HABIT

1	-	-	-	5	6	-	-	-	-	-	-	-	-	-	-	-	-	-	20	21	-	-	-	25	26	-	-	-	30	31	-	-	-	-	-	-	-	-	60
5 menses					55 tuhr																																		

SITUATION

1	-	-	-	5	6	-	-	-	-	-	-	-	-	-	-	-	-	-	20	21	-	-	-	25	26	-	-	-	30	31
5 blood					15 tuhr															11 blood										

1. *Analysis of the Situation*
    1. The blood from day 1 to day 5 is menstruation in keeping with her habit.
    2. The tuhr from day 6 to day 20 is a complete tuhr.
    3. The blood from day 21 to day 31 is invalid blood because it exceeds 10 days. No blood appears in the place of the habit.

2. *Solution*
    1. Since the blood exceeds 10 days, she returns to her menstrual habit.
        a) The place of the habit changes because there is no minimal amount in the habitual place.
        b) The number of days remains (i.e. 5 days), and it begins with the bleeding on day 21.
    2. The tuhr habit changes to 15 days because it is a valid tuhr.
    3. Day 1 to day 5 is menstruation.
    4. Day 6 to day 20 is tuhr.
    5. Day 21 to day 25 is menstruation.
    6. Day 26 to day 31 is istihada.

SOLUTION

																				new habit place										
1	-	-	-	5	6	-	-	-	-	-	-	-	-	-	-	-	-	-	20	21	-	-	-	25	26	-	-	-	30	31
5 menses					15 tuhr															5 menses					6 istihada					

3. *Rulings for the Day-by-Day Situation*

    1. With the appearance of blood on day 1, it is unlawful to pray or fast.
    2. When the blood stops on day 6, she is required to take a purificatory bath (ghusl), pray, and fast if Ramadan.
    3. With the return of blood on day 21, she stops praying and fasting because it is preceded by a complete tuhr.
    4. At the end of 10 complete days of bleeding on day 30, she is required to take a bath (ghusl), pray, and fast even if the bleeding continues.
    5. On day 31, it is clear that the bleeding exceeds the maximum, and thus the day-by-day rulings for this situation need to be revised.

4. *Revision of the Day-by-Day Rulings*

    1. Since the blood exceeds 10 days, she returns to her menstrual habit.
    2. There is no minimum in the place of the habit. Thus, the habit changes in terms of place and the number of days remains (i.e. 5 days).
    3. Day 26 to day 30:

        The ruling of menstruation is canceled and based on this:

        a) She must make up the prayers omitted, though there is no sin for not having prayed them.

        b) She must make up the fast-days if in Ramadan, though there is no sin for not having fasted these days.

5. *Precepts Applied for This Situation*

    1. It is obligatory for each woman to record her menstrual, lochial, and tuhr periods.
    2. It is obligatory to stop praying and fasting as soon as any bleeding occurs after a complete tuhr unless the bleeding occurs before the habit and if what remains of the tuhr-days added to the menstrual habit exceeds 10 days (dis: 11.51).

3. Each time the blood stops before 3 days, she prays with ablution. Each time it stops after 3 days, she prays with a purificatory bath (ghusl).
4. A complete tuhr separates between two bloods. The blood before and after this tuhr are considered menstruation if they reach the minimum and there is nothing else prohibiting it.
5. If real or legal blood exceeds 10 days, and there is no minimum in the habitual place, then the place changes, and the number remains the same from the onset of the blood and the rest is istihada.
6. If real or legal blood stops before 3 days or after 10 days, for someone with a habit, it is obligatory to make up the missed prayers.
7. The habit changes with a valid blood or a valid tuhr.

Notes

Menstrual Case One

Case Two

SITUATION: A woman has a 5-day menstrual habit and a 55-day tuhr habit. She has her usual 5 days of menstruation, then 64 days of tuhr, and then 11 days of blood.

HABIT

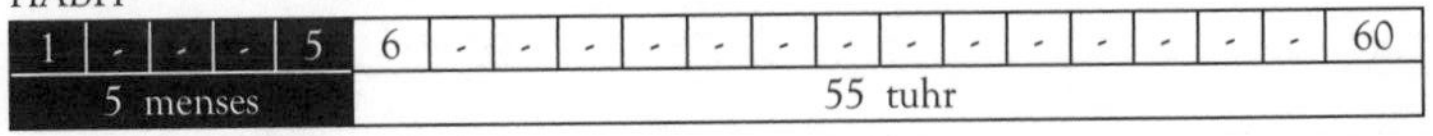

1	-	-	-	5	6	-	-	-	-	-	-	-	-	-	-	-	-	-	-	60
5 menses					55 tuhr															

SITUATION

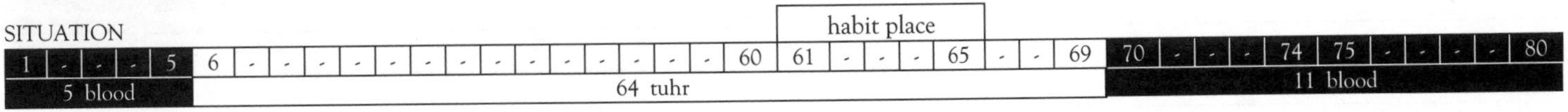

1	-	-	-	5	6	-	-	-	-	-	-	-	-	-	-	-	-	-	-	60	61 (habit place)	-	-	-	65	-	-	69	70	-	-	-	74	75	-	-	-	-	80
5 blood					64 tuhr																								11 blood										

1. *Analysis of the Situation*
    1. The blood from day 1 to day 5 is menstruation in keeping with her habit.
    2. The tuhr from day 6 to day 69 is a complete tuhr.
    3. The blood from day 70 to day 80 is invalid blood because it exceeds 10 days. No blood appears in the place of the habit.

2. *Solution*
    1. Since the blood exceeds 10 days, she returns to her menstrual habit.
        a) The place of habit changes because there is no minimal amount in its place.
        b) The number of days remains (i.e. 5 days), and it begins with the bleeding on day 70.
    2. The tuhr habit changes to 64 days because it is a valid tuhr.
    3. Day 1 to day 5 is menstruation.
    4. Day 6 to day 69 is tuhr.
    5. Day 70 to day 74 is menstruation.
    6. Day 75 to day 80 is istihada.

SOLUTION

			new habit place	
1 - - - 5	6 - - - - - - - - - - - - - - 60	61 - - - 65 - - 69	70 - - - 74	75 - - - - 80
5 menses	64 tuhr		5 menses	6 istihada

3. *Rulings for the Day-by-Day Situation*

    1. With the appearance of blood on day 1, it is unlawful to pray and fast.
    2. When the blood stops on day 6, she is required to take a purificatory bath (ghusl), to pray, and fast if Ramadan.
    3. Upon bleeding on day 70, she stops praying and fasting.
    4. At the end of 10 complete days of bleeding (i.e. day 79), she is required to take a bath (ghusl), pray, and fast even if the bleeding continues.
    5. On day 80, it is clear that the bleeding exceeds the maximum; thus, the day-by-day rulings for this situation need to be revised.

4. *Revision of the Day-by-Day Rulings*

    1. Since the blood exceeds 10 days, she returns to her menstrual habit.
    2. There is no minimum in the place of the habit. Thus, the habit changes in terms of place and the number of days remains (i.e. 5 days).
    3. Day 75 to day 79:

        The ruling of menstruation is canceled and based on this:

        a) She must make up the prayers omitted, though there is no sin for not having prayed them.
        b) She must make up the fast-days if in Ramadan, though there is no sin for not having fasted these days.

5. *Precepts Applied for This Situation*

    1. It is obligatory for each woman to record her menstrual, lochial, and tuhr periods.
    2. It is obligatory to stop praying and fasting as soon as any bleeding occurs after a complete tuhr unless the bleeding occurs before the habit and if what remains of the tuhr-days added to the menstrual habit exceeds 10 days.

Menstrual Case Two

3. Each time the blood stops before 3 days, she prays with ablution. Each time it stops after 3 days, she prays with a purificatory bath (ghusl).
4. A complete tuhr separates between two bloods. The blood before and after this tuhr are considered menstruation if they reach the minimum and there is nothing else prohibiting it.
5. If real or legal blood exceeds 10 days, and there is no minimum in the habitual place, then the place changes, and the number remains the same from the onset of the blood and the rest is istihada.
6. If real or legal blood stops before 3 days or after 10 days, for someone with a habit, it is obligatory to make up the missed prayers.
7. The habit changes with a valid blood or a valid tuhr.

Notes

Menstrual Case Two

Case Three

SITUATION: A woman has a 5-day menstrual habit and a 55-day tuhr habit. She has her usual 5 days of menstruation, then 46 days of tuhr, and then 11 days of blood.

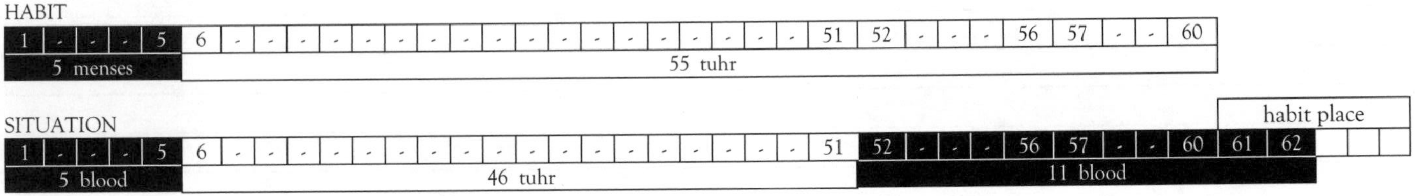

HABIT

1 - - - 5 | 6 - - - - - - - - - - - - - - - - - - 51 52 - - - 56 57 - - 60

5 menses | 55 tuhr

SITUATION

habit place (days 61–65)

1 - - - 5 | 6 - - - - - - - - - - - - - - - - - - 51 | 52 - - - 56 57 - - 60 61 62

5 blood | 46 tuhr | 11 blood

1. *Analysis of the Situation*
   1. The blood from day 1 to day 5 is menstruation in keeping with her habit.
   2. The tuhr from day 6 to day 51 is a complete tuhr.
   3. The blood from day 52 to day 62 is invalid blood because it exceeds 10 days.
      a) 9 days appear in the place of tuhr habit from day 52 to day 60.
      b) Only 2 days out of the required minimal amount appears in the habitual place (day 61 and day 62).
2. *Solution*
   1. Since the blood exceeds 10 days, she returns to her menstrual habit.
      a) The place of the habit changes because only 2 days appear in its habitual place (day 61 and day 62) and they are less than the minimal amount. Thus, it is not possible to make them a menstruation period.
      b) The number of days remains (i.e. 5 days) and begins with the bleeding on day 52.
   2. The tuhr habit changes to 46 days because it is a valid tuhr.
   3. Day 1 to day 5 is menstruation.
   4. Day 6 to day 51 is tuhr.

5. Day 52 to day 56 is menstruation.
6. Day 57 to day 62 is istihada.

SOLUTION

		new habit place	
1 | - | - | - | 5	6 | - | - | - | - | - | - | - | - | - | - | - | - | - | - | - | - | - | - | - | - | - | 51	52 | - | - | - | 56	57 | - | - | 60 | 61 | 62
5 menses	46 tuhr	5 menses	6 istihada

3. *Rulings for the Day-by-Day Situation*

1. With the appearance of blood on day 1, it is unlawful to pray and fast.
2. When the blood stops on day 6, she is required to take a purificatory bath (ghusl), to pray, and fast if Ramadan.
3. Upon bleeding on day 52, she continues praying and fasting because what remains from the days of her tuhr habit from day 52 to day 60 added to her menstrual habit in its habitual place exceeds 10 days.
4. It is precautionary that she take a bath (ghusl) on day 56, as it would be at the end of her 5-day menstrual habit in terms of the number of days, even if she were still bleeding because of the possibility of the habit changing its place.
5. On day 61, she stops praying and fasting because this is the first day of the habitual place of her menstrual habit and there is bleeding.
6. With the cessation of blood on day 62 three matters are made certain:
    a) The bleeding has exceeded the maximum.
    b) There is no minimal amount in its habitual place.
    c) She is obliged to take a bath (ghusl) if she did not take one on day 56, and thus the day-by-day rulings for this situation need to be revised.

4. *Revision of the Day-by-Day Rulings*

1. She returns to her menstrual habit because the bleeding exceeds 10 days.
2. Only 2 days occurred in their habitual place (day 61 and day 62), which is less than the minimum; thus, it is not possible to consider them menstruation. Therefore, the place changes but the number of days remains the same, which is 5 days from the start of the bleeding on day 52.

3. Day 52 to day 56:
   The ruling of tuhr is canceled and based on this:
   - a) Prayers are invalid because she prayed while in legal menstruation, though there is no sin for having done so. She need not repeat the prayers unless they were make-up prayers or a vowed prayer; then she must repeat them.
   - b) If she fasted an obligatory or wajib fast, she must make them up, though there is no sin upon her for having fasted.
4. Day 57 to 60:
   1) Her fasts are valid.
   2) The validity of the prayers depends on the following:
      - a) If she took a precautionary bath (ghusl) on day 56, then her prayers are valid.
      - b) If she did not take a bath (ghusl), then the prayers are invalid and she must repeat them.
5. Day 61 to day 62:
   The ruling of menstruation is canceled and based on this:
   - a) She is obliged to make up the prayers omitted, though there is no sin for not having prayed them.
   - b) She must make up the fast-days if in Ramadan, though there is no sin for not having fasted them.

5. *Precepts Applied for This Situation*

1. It is obligatory for each woman to record her menstrual, lochial, and tuhr periods.
2. It is obligatory to stop praying and fasting as soon as any bleeding occurs after a complete tuhr unless the bleeding occurs before the habit and if what remains of the tuhr-days added to the menstrual habit exceeds 10 days.
3. Each time the blood stops before 3 days, she prays with ablution. Each time it stops after 3 days, she prays with a purificatory bath (ghusl).
4. A complete tuhr separates between two bloods. The blood before and after this tuhr are considered menstruation if they reach the minimum and there is nothing else prohibiting it.
5. If real or legal blood exceeds 10 days, and there is no minimum in the habitual place, then the place changes, and the number remains the same from the onset of the blood and the rest is istihada.
6. If real or legal blood stops before 3 days or after 10 days, for someone with a habit, it is obligatory to make up the missed prayers.
7. The habit changes with a valid blood or a valid tuhr.

Notes

Menstrual Case Three

Case Four

SITUATION: A woman has a 5-day menstrual habit and a 55-day tuhr habit. She has her usual 5 days of menstruation, then 48 days of tuhr, and then 12 days of blood.

HABIT

1	-	-	-	5	6	-	-	-	-	-	-	-	-	-	-	-	-	-	-	-	-	-	-	-	-	-	53	54	-	-	-	-	-	60
5 menses					55 tuhr																													

SITUATION

																																			habit place				
1	-	-	-	5	6	-	-	-	-	-	-	-	-	-	-	-	-	-	-	-	-	-	-	-	-	-	53	54	-	-	-	-	-	60	61	-	-	-	65
5 blood					48 tuhr																							12 blood											

1. *Analysis of the Situation*
    1. The blood from day 1 to day 5 is menstruation in keeping with her habit.
    2. The tuhr from day 6 to day 53 is a complete tuhr.
    3. The blood from day 54 to day 65 is invalid blood because it exceeds 10 days.
        a) 7 days appear in the place of the tuhr habit from day 54 to day 60.
        b) 5 days appear in the habitual place of the menstrual habit from day 61 to day 65.

2. *Solution*
    1. Since the blood exceeds 10 days, she returns to her menstrual habit.
    2. The habit returns to its original place and number because the required minimal amount occurred in its habitual place. Thus, the bleeding that occurred in the place of the menstrual habit is menstruation and the rest is istihada.
    3. The tuhr habit remains because this tuhr is invalid since she prayed during 7 days of blood from day 54 to day 60.
    4. Day 1 to day 5 is menstruation.

5. Day 6 to day 53 is tuhr.
6. Day 54 to day 60 is istihada.
7. Day 61 to day 65 is menstruation.

SOLUTION

																																			habit place				
1	-	-	-	5	6	-	-	-	-	-	-	-	-	-	-	-	-	-	-	-	-	-	-	-	-	-	53	54	-	-	-	-	60	61	-	-	-	65
5 menses					55 tuhr																													5 menses				

3. *Rulings for the Day-by-Day Situation*

1. With the appearance of blood on day 1, it is unlawful to pray and fast.
2. When the blood stops on day 6, she is required to take a purificatory bath (ghusl), to pray, and fast if Ramadan.
3. Upon bleeding on day 54, she continues praying and fasting because what remains from the days of her tuhr habit from day 54 to day 60 added to her menstrual habit in its habitual place exceeds 10 days.
4. On day 61, she stops praying and fasting because this is the first day of the habitual place and there is bleeding.
5. With the cessation of blood on day 65, she is required to take a purificatory bath (ghusl), to pray, and fast.
6. On day 65, two matters are made certain:
   a) The bleeding has exceeded the maximum;
   b) There is the minimal amount in its habitual place that equals the menstrual habit of 5 days.
7. There is no change in the habit. The blood that occurred in the habitual place is menstruation and the rest is istihada.

4. *Precepts Applied for This Situation*

1. It is obligatory for each woman to record her menstrual, lochial, and tuhr periods.
2. It is obligatory to stop praying and fasting as soon as any bleeding occurs after a complete tuhr unless the bleeding occurs before the habit and if what remains of the tuhr-days added to the menstrual habit exceeds 10 days.

3. Each time the blood stops before 3 days, she prays with ablution. Each time it stops after 3 days, she prays with a purificatory bath (ghusl).
4. A complete tuhr separates between two bloods. The blood before and after this tuhr are considered menstruation if they reach the minimum and there is nothing else prohibiting it.
5. If real or legal blood exceeds 10 days, and a minimum occurs in the habitual place, equal to the habit, then the habit remains the same and the rest is istihada.
6. If real or legal blood stops before 3 days or after 10 days, for someone with a habit, it is obligatory to make up the missed prayers.
7. The habit changes with a valid blood or a valid tuhr.

Notes

Case Five

SITUATION: A woman has a 5-day menstrual habit and a 55-day tuhr habit. She has her usual 5 days of menses, then 54 days of tuhr, then 1 day of blood, then 14 days of tuhr, and then 1 day of blood.

HABIT

1	-	-	-	5	6	-	-	-	-	-	-	-	-	-	-	-	-	-	-	-	-	-	59	60
5 menses					55 tuhr																			

SITUATION

																									habit place														
1	-	-	-	5	6	-	-	-	-	-	-	-	-	-	-	-	-	-	-	-	-	-	59	60	61	-	-	-	65	66	-	-	-	-	-	-	-	74	75
5 blood					54 tuhr																			b	14 tuhr														b

1. *Analysis of the Situation*
    1. The blood from day 1 to day 5 is menstruation in keeping with her habit.
    2. The tuhr from day 6 to day 59 is a complete tuhr.
    3. The blood on day 60 is invalid blood because it is less than the minimum.
    4. The tuhr from day 61 to day 74 is an invalid tuhr because it is less than 15 days and does not separate between day 60 and day 75. This tuhr is legal blood, and it is added to the blood before and after it.
    5. The blood on day 75 is invalid blood that is added to the previous real and legal blood.
    6. The total days of blood that followed the complete tuhr is 16 days, of which 5 days appeared in its habitual place from day 61 to day 65.
2. *Solution*
    1. Since the blood exceeds 10 days, she returns to her menstrual habit.
    2. The habit returns to its original place and number because the minimal amount equal to it occurred in its habitual place. Thus, the legal blood that occurred in the place of the menstrual habit is menstruation and the rest is istihada.
    3. The tuhr habit remains because this tuhr is invalid, and it is not taken into consideration in changing the habit because it is mixed

with blood at the end of it on day 60.

4. Day 1 to day 5 is menstruation.
5. Day 6 to day 59 is tuhr.
6. Day 60 is istihada and completes the number of the tuhr habit.
7. Day 61 to day 65 is menstruation in accordance with the habit.
8. Day 66 to day 75 is istihada.

SOLUTION

																									habit place														
1	-	-	-	5	6	-	-	-	-	-	-	-	-	-	-	-	-	-	-	-	-	-	59	60	61	-	-	-	65	66	-	-	-	-	-	-	-	74	75
5 menses					55 tuhr																				5 menses					10 istihada									

3. *Rulings for the Day-by-Day Situation*

1. With the appearance of blood on day 1, it is unlawful to pray and fast.
2. When the blood stops on day 6, she is required to take a purificatory bath (ghusl), to pray, and fast if Ramadan.
3. Upon bleeding on day 60, she stops praying and fasting.
4. The cessation of bleeding on day 61 makes clear that the blood on day 60 is istihada. Thus, she must make up the prayers omitted with ablution and not a bath (ghusl), though there is no sin for leaving the prayer that day. If the day coincided with Ramadan, she must make up the fast-day, though there is no sin for not fasting that day.
5. It is precautionary that she take a bath (ghusl) on day 65, as it would be at the end of her 5-day menstrual habit in its habitual place, even if there is no bleeding because of the possibility of the habit changing its place.
6. Upon bleeding on day 75 it is clear that the previous tuhr is incomplete and does not separate between two bloods; rather it joins them.
    a) The total days of blood from day 60 to day 75 exceeds the maximum.

b) She is obliged to take a bath (ghusl) if she did not take the precautionary one on day 65. Thus, the day-by-day rulings for this situation need to be revised.

7. On day 75, she must continue praying and fasting since the blood is istihada because it follows an incomplete tuhr.

4. *Revision of the Day-by-Day Rulings*

1. She returns to her menstrual habit because the bleeding exceeds 10 days.
2. In the habitual place, from day 61 to day 65, is legal blood that equals the habit. Therefore, there is no change in the habit. Thus, the legal blood during the menstrual habit is menstruation and the rest is istihada.
3. Day 61 to day 65:

   The ruling of tuhr is canceled and based on this:

   a) Prayers are invalid because she prayed while in legal menstruation, though there is no sin for having done so. She need not repeat the prayers unless they were make-up prayers or a vowed prayer; then she must repeat them. Note: if she made up the prayers of day 60 during this time, she must repeat them again.

   b) If she fasted an obligatory or wajib fast, she must make them up, though there is no sin upon her for having fasted.

4. Day 66 to day 75:

   1) Her fasts are valid.

   2) The validity of her prayers depends on the following:

   a) If she took a precautionary bath (ghusl) on day 65, then her prayers are valid;

   b) If she did not take a precautionary bath (ghusl), then she is obliged to take a ghusl as soon as the bleeding begins and the previous prayers are invalid and must be repeated.

5. *Precepts Applied for This Situation*

1. It is obligatory for each woman to record her menstrual, lochial, and tuhr periods.

2. It is obligatory to stop praying and fasting as soon as any bleeding occurs after a complete tuhr unless the bleeding occurs before the habit and if what remains of the tuhr-days added to the menstrual habit exceeds 10 days.
3. Each time the blood stops before 3 days, she prays with ablution. Each time it stops after 3 days, she prays with a purificatory bath (ghusl).
4. A complete tuhr separates between two bloods. The blood before and after this tuhr are considered menstruation if they reach the minimum and there is nothing else prohibiting it.
5. If real or legal blood exceeds 10 days, and a minimum occurs in the habitual place, equal to the habit, then the habit remains the same and the rest is istihada.
6. If real or legal blood stops before 3 days or after 10 days, for someone with a habit, it is obligatory to make up the missed prayers.
7. An incomplete tuhr is considered legal blood that links the first actual bleeding to the second actual bleeding.
8. It is permissible for a woman with a habit to start and end a menstrual period with actual tuhr that is considered legal blood.
9. The purificatory bath (ghusl) is obligatory at the end of legal menstruation.
10. The habit changes with a valid blood or a valid tuhr.

Case Six

SITUATION: A woman has a 5-day menstrual habit and a 55-day tuhr habit. She has her usual 5 days of menstruation, then 57 days of tuhr, then 3 days of blood, then 14 days of tuhr, and then 1 day of blood.

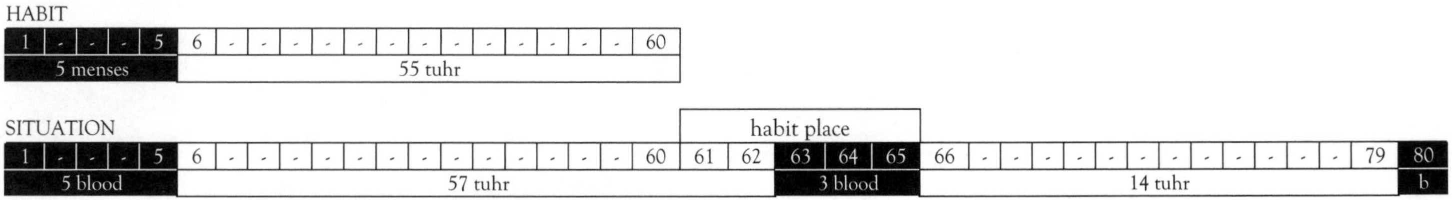

HABIT

1	-	-	-	5	6	-	-	-	-	-	-	-	-	-	-	-	-	-	60
5 menses					55 tuhr														

SITUATION

1	-	-	-	5	6	-	-	-	-	-	-	-	-	-	-	-	-	-	60	61	62	63	64	65	66	-	-	-	-	-	-	-	-	-	-	-	-	79	80
																				habit place																			
5 blood					57 tuhr																	3 blood			14 tuhr														b

1. *Analysis of the Situation*
    1. The blood from day 1 to day 5 is menstruation in keeping with her habit.
    2. The tuhr from day 6 to day 62 is a complete tuhr.
    3. The blood from day 63 to day 65:
        a) The blood is valid because it reaches the minimal amount and appears after a valid tuhr.
        b) The blood occurs in its habitual place but is less than the habit.
    4. The tuhr from day 66 to day 79 is an invalid tuhr because it is less than 15 days and does not separate between day 65 and day 80. This tuhr is legal blood, and it is added to the blood before and after it.
    5. The blood on day 80 is invalid and is added to the previous real and legal blood.
    6. The total of blood occurring after the complete tuhr is 18 days, 3 days of which occurred in its habitual place from day 63 to day 65.

2. *Solution*
    1. Since the blood exceeds 10 days, she returns to her menstrual habit.
        a) The place of the habit remains because the minimal amount occurred in it.

b) The number of the habit changes to 3 days because they occurred in the habitual place.

2. The tuhr habit changes to 57 days because it is a valid tuhr.
5. Day 1 to day 5 is menstruation in keeping with her habit.
6. Day 6 to day 62 is tuhr.
7. Day 63 to day 65 is menstruation.
8. Day 66 to day 80 is istihada.

SOLUTION

<table>
<tr><td colspan="5"></td><td colspan="17"></td><td colspan="3">habit place</td><td colspan="15"></td></tr>
<tr><td>1</td><td>-</td><td>-</td><td>-</td><td>5</td><td>6</td><td>-</td><td>-</td><td>-</td><td>-</td><td>-</td><td>-</td><td>-</td><td>-</td><td>-</td><td>-</td><td>-</td><td>-</td><td>-</td><td>60</td><td>61</td><td>62</td><td>63</td><td>64</td><td>65</td><td>66</td><td>-</td><td>-</td><td>-</td><td>-</td><td>-</td><td>-</td><td>-</td><td>-</td><td>-</td><td>-</td><td>-</td><td>-</td><td>79</td><td>80</td></tr>
<tr><td colspan="5">5 menses</td><td colspan="17">57 tuhr</td><td colspan="3">3 menses</td><td colspan="15">15 istihada</td></tr>
</table>

3. *Rulings for the Day-by-Day Situation*

1. With the appearance of blood on day 1, it is unlawful to pray and fast.
2. When the blood stops on day 6, she is required to take a purificatory bath (ghusl), to pray, and fast if Ramadan.
3. Upon bleeding on day 63, she stops praying and fasting.
4. With the cessation of blood on day 65, she takes a bath (ghusl), prays, and fasts.
5. The blood on day 80 makes it is clear that the previous tuhr was incomplete and it does not separate between the two bloods, thus exceeding the maximum. Therefore, the day-by-day rulings for this situation need to be revised.
6. On day 80, she must continue praying and fasting; the blood is istihada because it follows an incomplete tuhr.

4. *Revision of the Day-by-Day Rulings*

1. She returns to her menstrual habit because the bleeding exceeds 10 days.
2. A minimal amount occurs in the place of the habit that is less than the habit; thus, the habit changes to the 3 days that occurred in the habitual place.
3. In reviewing the situation, it is clear that no revision is needed because she stopped praying and fasting during the valid bleeding and took a bath (ghusl), prayed, and fasted in the days of tuhr.

5. *Precepts Applied for This Situation*

   1. It is obligatory for each woman to record her menstrual, lochial, and tuhr periods.
   2. It is obligatory to stop praying and fasting as soon as any bleeding occurs after a complete tuhr unless the bleeding occurs before the habit and if what remains of the tuhr-days added to the menstrual habit exceeds 10 days.
   3. Each time the blood stops before 3 days, she prays with ablution. Each time it stops after 3 days, she prays with a purificatory bath (ghusl).
   4. A complete tuhr separates between two bloods. The blood before and after this tuhr are considered menstruation if they reach the minimum and there is nothing else prohibiting it.
   5. An incomplete tuhr is considered legal blood that links the first actual bleeding to the second actual bleeding.
   6. The habit changes with a valid blood or a valid tuhr.
   7. If real or legal blood exceeds 10 days, and a minimum occurs in the habitual place but is less that the habit, then the number changes to those that have occurred in the proper place and becomes the new habit, while the rest is istihada.
   8. If real or legal blood stops before 3 days or after 10 days, for someone with a habit, it is obligatory to make up the missed prayers.

Notes

Menstrual Case Six

Case Seven

SITUATION: A woman has a 5-day menstrual habit and a 55-day tuhr habit. She has her usual 5 days of menstruation, then 55 days of tuhr, and then 9 days of blood.

HABIT

1	-	-	-	5	6	-	-	-	-	-	-	-	-	-	-	-	-	-	-	-	-	-	-	-	-	-	-	-	-	60
5 menses					55 tuhr																									

SITUATION

																															habit place								
1	-	-	-	5	6	-	-	-	-	-	-	-	-	-	-	-	-	-	-	-	-	-	-	-	-	-	-	-	-	60	61	-	-	-	65	66	-	-	69
5 blood					55 tuhr																										9 blood								

1. *Analysis of the Situation*

    1. The blood from day 1 to day 5 is menstruation in keeping with her habit.
    2. The tuhr from day 6 to day 60 is a complete tuhr.
    3. The blood from day 61 to day 69 is valid because it reaches the minimum and does not exceed the maximum and follows a valid tuhr:
        a) 5 days, which is more than the minimum, appear in the habitual place from day 61 to day 65.
        b) 4 days, which is more than the minimum, appears after the habit from day 66 to day 69.

2. *Solution*

    1. The menstrual habit changes to 9 days because it does not exceed the maximum if it is followed by a valid tuhr.
    2. Day 1 to day 5 is menstruation.
    3. Day 6 to day 60 is tuhr.
    4. Day 61 to day 69 is menstruation.

SOLUTION

																															habit place								
1	-	-	-	5	6	-	-	-	-	-	-	-	-	-	-	-	-	-	-	-	-	-	-	-	-	-	-	-	-	60	61	-	-	-	65	66	-	-	69
5 menses					55 tuhr																										9 menses								

3. *Rulings for the Day-by-Day Situation*

   1. With the appearance of blood on day 1, it is unlawful to pray and fast.
   2. When the blood stops on day 6, she is required to take a purificatory bath (ghusl), to pray, and fast if Ramadan.
   3. Upon bleeding on day 61, she stops praying and fasting.
   4. When the blood stops on day 69, she is required to take a bath (ghusl), to pray, and fast.

4. *Precepts Applied for This Situation*

   1. It is obligatory for each woman to record her menstrual, lochial, and tuhr periods.
   2. It is obligatory to stop praying and fasting as soon as any bleeding occurs after a complete tuhr unless the bleeding occurs before the habit and if what remains of the tuhr-days added to the menstrual habit exceeds 10 days.
   3. Each time the blood stops before 3 days, she prays with ablution. Each time it stops after 3 days, she prays with a purificatory bath (ghusl).
   4. A complete tuhr separates between two bloods. The blood before and after this tuhr are considered menstruation if they reach the minimum and there is nothing else prohibiting it.
   5. If the blood does not exceed 10 days, then all of it is menses provided there is a valid tuhr after it.
   6. The habit changes with a valid blood or a valid tuhr.

Case Eight

SITUATION: A woman has a 5-day menstrual habit and a 55-day tuhr habit. She has her usual 5 days of menstruation, then 50 days of tuhr, and then 10 days of blood.

HABIT

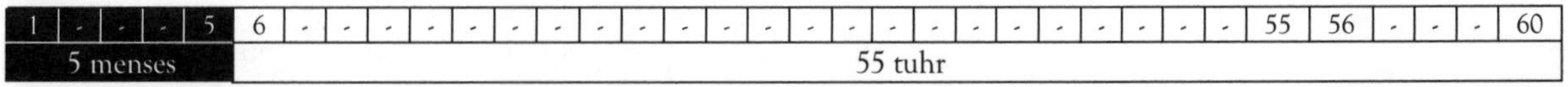

1 - - - 5 | 6 - 55 56 - - - 60

5 menses | 55 tuhr

SITUATION

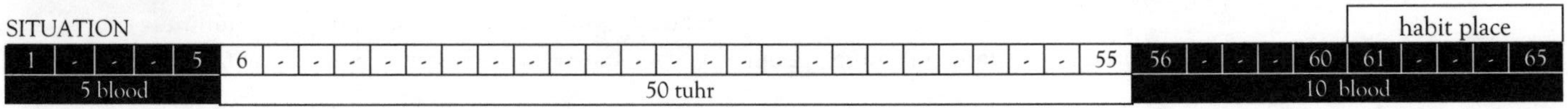

habit place

1 - - - 5 | 6 - 55 | 56 - - - 60 61 - - - 65

5 blood | 50 tuhr | 10 blood

1. *Analysis of the Situation*

   1. The blood from day 1 to day 5 is menstruation in keeping with her habit.
   2. The tuhr from day 6 to day 55 is a complete tuhr.
   3. The blood from day 56 to day 65 is valid blood because it reaches the minimum and does not exceed the maximum and follows a valid tuhr:
      a) 5 days, which is more than the minimum, appear before the habit from day 56 to day 60.
      b) 5 days in the place of the habit and equal to the habit appear from day 61 to day 65.

2. *Solution*

   1. The menstrual habit changes to 10 days because it does not exceed the maximum if it is followed by a valid tuhr.
   2. The tuhr habit changes to 50 days.
   3. Day 1 to day 5 is menstruation.
   4. Day 6 to day 55 is tuhr.
   5. Day 56 to day 65 is menstruation.

SOLUTION

<table>
<tr><td colspan="30"></td><td colspan="10">habit place</td></tr>
<tr><td>1</td><td>-</td><td>-</td><td>-</td><td>5</td><td>6</td><td>-</td><td>-</td><td>-</td><td>-</td><td>-</td><td>-</td><td>-</td><td>-</td><td>-</td><td>-</td><td>-</td><td>-</td><td>-</td><td>-</td><td>-</td><td>-</td><td>-</td><td>-</td><td>-</td><td>-</td><td>-</td><td>-</td><td>-</td><td>55</td><td>56</td><td>-</td><td>-</td><td>-</td><td>60</td><td>61</td><td>-</td><td>-</td><td>-</td><td>65</td></tr>
<tr><td colspan="5">5 menses</td><td colspan="25">50 tuhr</td><td colspan="10">10 menses</td></tr>
</table>

3. *Rulings for the Day-by-Day Situation*

    1. With the appearance of blood on day 1, it is unlawful to pray and fast.
    2. When the blood stops on day 6, she is required to take a purificatory bath (ghusl), to pray, and fast if Ramadan.
    3. Upon bleeding on day 56, she stops praying and fasting.
    4. When the blood stops on day 65, she is required to take a bath (ghusl), to pray, and fast.

4. *Precepts Applied for This Situation*

    1. It is obligatory for each woman to record her menstrual, lochial, and tuhr periods.
    2. It is obligatory to stop praying and fasting as soon as any bleeding occurs after a complete tuhr unless the bleeding occurs before the habit and if what remains of the tuhr-days added to the menstrual habit exceeds 10 days.
    3. Each time the blood stops before 3 days, she prays with ablution. Each time it stops after 3 days, she prays with a purificatory bath (ghusl).
    4. A complete tuhr separates between two bloods. The blood before and after this tuhr are considered menstruation if they reach the minimum and there is nothing else prohibiting it.
    5. If the blood does not exceed 10 days, then all of it is menses provided there is a valid tuhr after it.
    6. The habit changes with a valid blood or a valid tuhr.

Case Nine

SITUATION: A woman has a 5-day menstrual habit and a 55-day tuhr habit. She has her usual 5 days of menstruation, then 54 days of tuhr, and then 8 days of blood.

HABIT

1	-	-	-	5	6	-	-	-	-	-	-	-	-	-	-	-	-	-	-	-	-	-	-	-	-	-	-	-	-	59	60
5 menses					55 tuhr																										

SITUATION

																															habit place						
1	-	-	-	5	6	-	-	-	-	-	-	-	-	-	-	-	-	-	-	-	-	-	-	-	-	-	-	-	-	59	60	61	-	-	-	65	66	67
5 blood					54 tuhr																										8 blood							

1. *Analysis of the Situation*

1. The blood from day 1 to day 5 is menstruation in keeping with her habit.
2. The tuhr from day 6 to day 59 is a complete tuhr.
3. The blood from day 60 to day 67 is valid blood because it reaches the minimum, does not exceed the maximum, and follows a valid tuhr:
    a) 1 day appears before the habit from day 56 to day 60 that is less than the minimum.
    b) 5 days in the place of the habit and equal to the habit appear from day 61 to day 65.
    c) 2 days appear after the habit from day 66 to day 67 that is less than the minimum.

2. *Solution*

1. The menstrual habit changes to 8 days because it does not exceed the maximum if it is followed by a valid tuhr.
2. The tuhr habit changes to 54 days.
3. Day 1 to day 5 is menstruation.

4. Day 6 to day 59 is tuhr.
5. Day 60 to day 67 is menstruation.

SOLUTION

																															habit place							
1	-	-	-	5	6	-	-	-	-	-	-	-	-	-	-	-	-	-	-	-	-	-	-	-	-	-	-	-	-	59	60	61	-	-	-	65	66	67
5 menses					54 tuhr																										8 menses							

3. *Rulings for the Day-by-Day Situation*

   1. With the appearance of blood on day 1, it is unlawful to pray and fast.
   2. When the blood stops on day 6, she is required to take a purificatory bath (ghusl), to pray, and fast if Ramadan.
   3. Upon bleeding on day 60, she stops praying and fasting.
   4. When the blood stops on day 67, she is required to take a bath (ghusl), to pray, and fast.

4. *Precepts Applied for This Situation*

   1. It is obligatory for each woman to record her menstrual, lochial, and tuhr periods.
   2. It is obligatory to stop praying and fasting as soon as any bleeding occurs after a complete tuhr unless the bleeding occurs before the habit and if what remains of the tuhr-days added to the menstrual habit exceeds 10 days.
   3. Each time the blood stops before 3 days, she prays with ablution. Each time it stops after 3 days, she prays with a purificatory bath (ghusl).
   4. A complete tuhr separates between two bloods. The blood before and after this tuhr are considered menstruation if they reach the minimum and there is nothing else prohibiting it.
   5. If the blood does not exceed 10 days, then all of it is menses provided there is a valid tuhr after it.
   6. The habit changes with a valid blood or a valid tuhr.

Case Ten

SITUATION: A woman has a 5-day menstrual habit and a 55-day tuhr habit. She has her usual 5 days of menstruation, then 50 days of tuhr, and then 7 days of blood.

HABIT

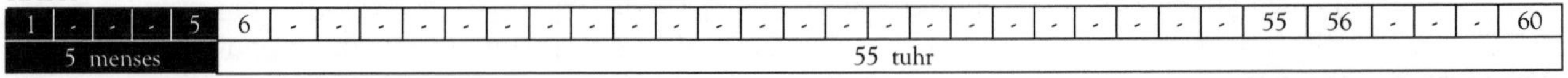

1 - - - 5	6 - - - … - - - 55 56 - - - 60
5 menses	55 tuhr

SITUATION

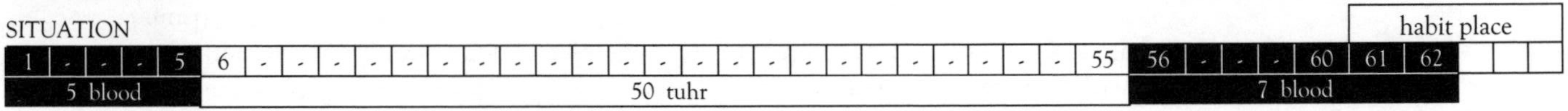

1 - - - 5	6 - - - … - - - 55	56 - - - 60 61 62
5 blood	50 tuhr	7 blood

habit place (day 61 onward)

1. *Analysis of the Situation*
   1. The blood from day 1 to day 5 is menstruation in keeping with her habit.
   2. The tuhr from day 6 to day 55 is a complete tuhr.
   3. The blood from day 56 to day 62 is valid blood because it reaches the minimum and follows a valid tuhr:
      a) 5 days appear before the habit and are equal to the habit from day 56 to day 60.
      b) 2 days appear in the place of the habit from day 61 to day 65 that is less than the minimum.

2. *Solution*
   1. The menstrual habit changes to 7 days because it does not exceed the maximum if it is followed by a valid tuhr.
   2. The tuhr habit changes to 50 days.
   3. Day 1 to day 5 is menstruation.
   4. Day 6 to day 55 is tuhr.
   5. Day 56 to day 62 is menstruation.

SOLUTION

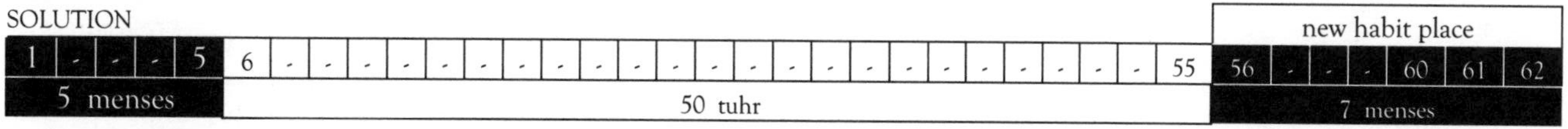

																														new habit place						
1	-	-	-	5	6	-	-	-	-	-	-	-	-	-	-	-	-	-	-	-	-	-	-	-	-	-	-	-	55	56	-	-	-	60	61	62
5 menses					50 tuhr																									7 menses						

3. *Rulings for the Day-by-Day Situation*

    1. With the appearance of blood on day 1, it is unlawful to pray and fast.
    2. When the blood stops on day 6, she is required to take a purificatory bath (ghusl), to pray, and fast if Ramadan.
    3. Upon bleeding on day 56, she stops praying and fasting.
    4. When the blood stops on day 62, she is required to take a bath (ghusl), to pray, and fast.

4. *Precepts Applied for This Situation*

    1. It is obligatory for each woman to record her menstrual, lochial, and tuhr periods.
    2. It is obligatory to stop praying and fasting as soon as any bleeding occurs after a complete tuhr unless the bleeding occurs before the habit and if what remains of the tuhr-days added to the menstrual habit exceeds 10 days.
    3. Each time the blood stops before 3 days, she prays with ablution. Each time it stops after 3 days, she prays with a purificatory bath (ghusl).
    4. A complete tuhr separates between two bloods. The blood before and after this tuhr are considered menstruation if they reach the minimum and there is nothing else prohibiting it.
    5. If the blood does not exceed 10 days, then all of it is menses provided there is a valid tuhr after it.
    6. The habit changes with a valid blood or a valid tuhr.

Case Eleven

SITUATION: A woman has a 5-day menstrual habit and a 55-day tuhr habit. She has her usual 5 days of menstruation, then 58 days of tuhr, and then 3 days of blood.

HABIT

1	-	-	-	5	6	-	-	-	-	-	-	-	-	-	-	-	-	-	-	-	-	-	-	-	-	-	-	-	-	-	-	60
5 menses					55 tuhr																											

SITUATION

																																	habit place					
1	-	-	-	5	6	-	-	-	-	-	-	-	-	-	-	-	-	-	-	-	-	-	-	-	-	-	-	-	-	-	-	60	61	62	63	64	65	66
5 blood					58 tuhr																															3 blood		

1. *Analysis of the Situation*
    1. The blood from day 1 to day 5 is menstruation in keeping with her habit.
    2. The tuhr from day 6 to day 63 is a complete tuhr.
    3. The blood from day 64 to day 66 is valid blood because it reaches the minimum, does not exceed the maximum, and follows a valid tuhr:
        a) 2 days appear in the place of the habit from day 64 and day 65 that are less than the minimum.
        b) 1 day appears after the habit, day 66, which is less than the minimum.

2. *Solution*
    1. The menstrual habit changes to 3 days because it does not exceed the maximum if it is followed by a valid tuhr.
    2. The tuhr habit changes to 58 days.
    3. Day 1 to day 5 is menstruation.
    4. Day 6 to day 63 is tuhr.
    5. Day 64 to day 66 is menstruation.

SOLUTION

																																				new place		
1	-	-	-	5	6	-	-	-	-	-	-	-	-	-	-	-	-	-	-	-	-	-	-	-	-	-	-	-	-	-	-	60	61	62	63	64	65	66
5 menses					58 tuhr																															3 menses		

3. *Rulings for the Day-by-Day Situation*

    1. With the appearance of blood on day 1, it is unlawful to pray and fast.
    2. When the blood stops on day 6, she is required to take a purificatory bath (ghusl), to pray, and fast if Ramadan.
    3. Upon bleeding on day 64, she stops praying and fasting.
    4. When the blood stops on day 66, she is required to take a bath (ghusl), to pray, and fast.

4. *Precepts Applied for This Situation*

    1. It is obligatory for each woman to record her menstrual, lochial, and tuhr periods.
    2. It is obligatory to stop praying and fasting as soon as any bleeding occurs after a complete tuhr unless the bleeding occurs before the habit and if what remains of the tuhr-days added to the menstrual habit exceeds 10 days.
    3. Each time the blood stops before 3 days, she prays with ablution. Each time it stops after 3 days, she prays with a purificatory bath (ghusl).
    4. A complete tuhr separates between two bloods. The blood before and after this tuhr are considered menstruation if they reach the minimum and there is nothing else prohibiting it.
    5. If the blood does not exceed 10 days, then all of it is menses provided there is a valid tuhr after it.
    6. The habit changes with a valid blood or a valid tuhr.

Case Twelve

SITUATION: A woman has a 5-day menstrual habit and a 55-day tuhr habit. She has her usual 5 days of menstruation, then 64 days of tuhr, and then 7 days of blood.

HABIT

1 - - - 5 | 6 - - - - - - - - - - - - - - - - - 60
5 menses | 55 tuhr

SITUATION

habit place (61 - 65)

1 - - - 5 | 6 - - - - - - - - - - - - - - - - - 60 61 - - - 65 66 - - 69 | 70 - - - - - 76
5 blood | 64 tuhr | 7 blood

1. *Analysis of the Situation*
    1. The blood from day 1 to day 5 is menstruation in keeping with her habit.
    2. The tuhr from day 6 to day 69 is a complete tuhr.
    3. The blood from day 70 to day 76 is valid blood because it reaches the minimum, does not exceed the maximum, and follows a valid tuhr:
        a) No days appear before or during the habit.
        b) 7 days, which is more than the habit, appear after the place of the habit from day 70 to day 76.
2. *Solution*
    1. The menstrual habit changes to 7 days because it does not exceed the maximum if it is followed by a valid tuhr.
    2. The tuhr habit changes to 64 days.
    3. Day 1 to day 5 is menstruation.
    4. Day 6 to day 69 is tuhr.
    5. Day 70 to day 76 is menstruation.

SOLUTION

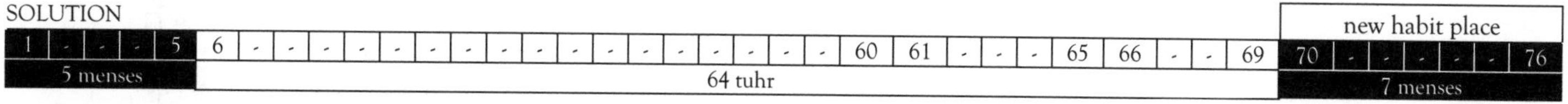

<table>
<tr><td colspan="33"></td><td colspan="7">new habit place</td></tr>
<tr><td>1</td><td>-</td><td>-</td><td>-</td><td>5</td><td>6</td><td>-</td><td>-</td><td>-</td><td>-</td><td>-</td><td>-</td><td>-</td><td>-</td><td>-</td><td>-</td><td>-</td><td>-</td><td>-</td><td>-</td><td>-</td><td>-</td><td>-</td><td>60</td><td>61</td><td>-</td><td>-</td><td>-</td><td>65</td><td>66</td><td>-</td><td>-</td><td>69</td><td>70</td><td>-</td><td>-</td><td>-</td><td>-</td><td>-</td><td>76</td></tr>
<tr><td colspan="5">5 menses</td><td colspan="28">64 tuhr</td><td colspan="7">7 menses</td></tr>
</table>

3. *Rulings for the Day-by-Day Situation*

   1. With the appearance of blood on day 1, it is unlawful to pray and fast.
   2. When the blood stops on day 6, she is required to take a purificatory bath (ghusl), to pray, and fast if Ramadan.
   3. Upon bleeding on day 70, she stops praying and fasting.
   4. When the blood stops on day 76, she is required to take a bath (ghusl), to pray, and fast.

4. *Precepts Applied for This Situation*

   1. It is obligatory for each woman to record her menstrual, lochial, and tuhr periods.
   2. It is obligatory to stop praying and fasting as soon as any bleeding occurs after a complete tuhr unless the bleeding occurs before the habit and if what remains of the tuhr-days added to the menstrual habit exceeds 10 days.
   3. Each time the blood stops before 3 days, she prays with ablution. Each time it stops after 3 days, she prays with a purificatory bath (ghusl).
   4. A complete tuhr separates between two bloods. The blood before and after this tuhr are considered menstruation if they reach the minimum and there is nothing else prohibiting it.
   5. If the blood does not exceed 10 days, then all of it is menses provided there is a valid tuhr after it.
   6. The habit changes with a valid blood or a valid tuhr.

Case Thirteen

SITUATION: A woman has a 20-day lochial habit, a 5-day menstrual habit, and a 17-day tuhr habit. She gives birth and has 1 day of blood, then 25 days of tuhr, then 1 day of blood, then 14 days of tuhr, and then 1 day of blood.

HABIT

1	2	-	-	-	-	-	-	-	-	-	-	-	-	-	-	-	-	-	20
20 lochia																			

SITUATION

1	2	-	-	-	-	-	-	-	-	-	-	-	-	-	-	-	-	-	20	21	-	-	26	27	28	-	-	-	-	-	-	37	38	39	40	41	42
b	25 tuhr																							b	14 tuhr												b

1. *Analysis of the Situation*
    1. The blood on day 1 is lochia given that it came after childbirth.
    2. The tuhr from day 2 to day 26 is a mixed tuhr, complete in terms of length, invalid because it occurs during the possible days of lochia. This tuhr is legal blood, and it is added to the blood before and after it.
    3. The blood on day 27 is added to all the previous blood: the 1 day of actual blood and the 25 days of legal blood.
    4. The tuhr from day 28 to day 41 is an invalid tuhr because it is less than 15 days and does not separate between day 27 and day 42. It is considered legal blood.
    5. The blood on day 42 is added to all the previous legal and actual blood.
    6. Total blood equals 42 days.
2. *Solution*
    1. She returns to her previous lochial habit because the bleeding exceeds 40 days.
    2. The first 20 days after giving birth is lochia: day 1 of actual blood and day 2 to 20 of legal blood.
    3. Day 21 to day 37 is tuhr in accordance with her 17-day tuhr habit.

4. Day 38 to day 42 is menstruation in accordance with her 5-day menstrual habit.

SOLUTION

<table>
<tr><td>1</td><td>2</td><td>-</td><td>-</td><td>-</td><td>-</td><td>-</td><td>-</td><td>-</td><td>-</td><td>-</td><td>-</td><td>-</td><td>-</td><td>-</td><td>-</td><td>-</td><td>-</td><td>-</td><td>20</td><td>21</td><td>-</td><td>-</td><td>26</td><td>27</td><td>28</td><td>-</td><td>-</td><td>-</td><td>-</td><td>-</td><td>-</td><td>37</td><td>38</td><td>39</td><td>40</td><td>41</td><td>42</td></tr>
<tr><td colspan="20">20 lochia</td><td colspan="13">17 tuhr</td><td colspan="5">5 menses</td></tr>
</table>

3. *Rulings for the Day-by-Day Situation*

1. Lochia begins after giving birth; it is unlawful to pray or fast.
2. When the blood stops on day 2, she is required to take a purificatory bath (ghusl), to pray, and fast if Ramadan.
3. Sexual intercourse is unlawful from day 2 to day 20 even though she is not bleeding because of the likelihood that the blood will return during its habitual time. However, she is required to pray, and fast.
4. It is precautionary that she take a bath (ghusl) at the end of her habit on day 20, even though she does not see blood because of the possibility of returning to her habit.
5. With the return of blood on day 27, she must stop praying and fasting.
6. The blood on day 27 invalidates the previous tuhr from day 2 to day 26 because it is a mixed tuhr.
7. When the blood stops on day 28, she is required to take a bath (ghusl), to pray and fast.
8. The blood on day 42 invalidates the previous tuhr from day 28 to day 41 because it is incomplete. Thus, the blood exceeds the 40 days maximum and the day-by-day rulings for this situation need to be revised.

4. *Revision of the Day-by-Day Rulings*

1. She returns to her lochial, tuhr and menstrual habits because the bleeding exceeds 40 days.
2. Day 2 to day 20:

   The ruling of tuhr is canceled and based on this:

   a) Prayers are invalid because she prayed while in legal lochia, though there is no sin for having done so. She need not repeat the prayers unless they were make-up prayers or a vowed prayer; then she must repeat them.

b) If she fasted an obligatory or wajib fast, she must make them up, though there is no sin upon her for having fasted.

3. Day 21 to day 37:

She returns to tuhr habit of 17 days, and based on this:

a) Day 21 to day 26:
   - Her fasts are valid.

b) The validity of her prayers depends on the following:
   - If she took a precautionary bath (ghusl) on day 20, then her prayers are valid.
   - If she did not take a precautionary bath (ghusl), then the prayers are invalid and must be repeated.

c) Day 27:
   - She must make up the prayers omitted, though there is no sin for not having prayed them.
   - She must make up the fast-day if in Ramadan, though there is no sin for not having fasted it.

d) Day 28 to day 37:
   - Her prayers and fasts are valid.

4. Day 38 to day 42:

She returns to her menstrual habit, and based on this:

a) The ruling of tuhr is canceled from day 38 to day 41.

b) Prayers are invalid because she prayed while in legal menstruation, though there is no sin for having done so. She need not repeat the prayers except if the prayers were make-up prayers or a vowed prayer; then she must repeat them.

c) If she fasted an obligatory or wajib fast, she must make them up, though there is no sin upon her for having fasted.

5. *Precepts Applied for This Situation*

1. It is obligatory for each woman to record her menstrual, lochial, and tuhr periods.

2. It is obligatory to stop ritual prayers and fast as soon as any bleeding occurs during the possible days of lochia.
3. It is obligatory to take a purificatory bath (ghusl) if the bleeding stops any time within the possible days of lochia.
4. Sexual intercourse is unlawful if the bleeding stops before the habit until the completion of the habit.
5. A mixed tuhr during the possible days of lochia is considered legal blood.
6. An incomplete tuhr is considered legal blood that links the first actual bleeding to the second actual bleeding.
7. If real or legal blood exceeds 40 days, she returns to her habit and all blood in excess of the habit is istihada.
8. If real or legal blood exceeds 40 days, for someone with a habit, it is obligatory to make up the prayers missed in excess of the habit.
9. It is permissible to end lochia with actual tuhr that is considered legal blood.
10. The purificatory bath (ghusl) is obligatory at the end of legal lochia.
11. Two lochial periods, or a lochial and menstrual period cannot succeed each other; there must be a complete tuhr between them.
12. The minimal tuhr interval between a lochial and menstrual period is 15 days.
13. It is permissible for a woman with a habit to start and end a menstrual period with actual tuhr that is considered legal blood.

Case Fourteen

SITUATION: A woman has a 7-day menstrual habit and 21-day tuhr habit. She has her usual 7 days of menstruation, then becomes pregnant and has 30 days of tuhr, then 15 days of blood, and then miscarries an embryo that has no discernible human features.

HABIT

1	-	-	-	7	8	-	-	-	-	-	-	-	-	-	-	-	28
7 menses					21 tuhr												

SITUATION

1	-	-	-	7	8	-	-	-	-	-	-	-	-	-	-	-	28	-	-	-	-	-	-	37	38	-	-	-	-	44	45	-	-	-	-	-	52	53
7 blood					30 tuhr																				15 blood													M

1. *Analysis of the Situation*
    1. The blood from day 1 to day 7 is menstruation in keeping with her habit.
    2. The tuhr from day 8 to day 37 is a complete tuhr.
    3. The blood from day 38 to day 52 is istihada because this is during pregnancy.
    4. The blood on day 53 is istihada because of the miscarried embryo.
2. *Solution*
    1. A miscarriage of an embryo nullifies pregnancy. Thus, she returns to her menstrual and tuhr habits.
    2. The tuhr habit changes to 30 days because it is valid.
    3. The place of the habit changes because there is no blood during it.
    4. The number of days remains and it begins with the bleeding on day 38.
    5. Day 1 to day 7 is menstruation.
    6. Day 8 to day 37 is tuhr.
    7. Day 38 to day 44 is menstruation.

8. Day 45 to day 53 is istihada.

SOLUTION

		new habit place	
1 - - - 7	8 - - - - - - - - - - - 28 - - - - - - 37	38 - - - - 44	45 - - - - - 52 53
7 menses	30 tuhr	7 menses	9 istihada

3. *Rulings for the Day-by-Day Situation*

1. With the appearance of blood on day 1, it is unlawful to pray and fast.
2. When the blood stops on day 8, she is required to take a purificatory bath (ghusl), to pray, and fast if Ramadan.
3. Upon bleeding on day 38, she continues praying and fasting because any blood during pregnancy is istihada.
4. On day 53 the legal status of pregnancy is canceled because of the miscarriage. The day-by-day rulings for this situation need to be revised.

4. *Revision of the Day-by-Day Rulings*

1. After the miscarriage, she returns to her menstrual and tuhr habits.
2. Day 38 to day 44:

    The ruling of tuhr is canceled and based on this:

    a) Prayers are invalid because she prayed while in legal menstruation, though there is no sin for having done so. She need not repeat the prayers unless they were make-up prayers or a vowed prayer; then she must repeat them.

    b) If she fasted an obligatory or wajib fast, she must make them up, though there is no sin upon her for having fasted.
3. Day 45 to day 53:

    1) Her fasts are valid.

    2) The validity of the prayers depends on the following:

    a) If she took a bath (ghusl) on day 45, then her prayers are valid.

b) If she did not take a bath (ghusl), then the prayers are invalid and she must repeat them.

3) After the miscarriage, she is obliged to pray and fast because the blood is istihada.

5. *Precepts Applied for This Situation*

1. It is obligatory for each woman to record her menstrual, lochial, and tuhr periods.
2. A pregnant woman does not menstruate. Any bleeding during pregnancy is istihada.
3. The blood before or after a miscarried embryo without discernible human features is menstruation if it reaches the minimum and comes after a complete tuhr.
4. If real or legal blood exceeds 10 days, and there is no minimum in the habitual place, then the place changes, and the number remains the same from the onset of the blood and the rest is istihada.
5. If real or legal blood stops before 3 days or after 10 days, for someone with a habit, it is obligatory to make up the missed prayers.
6. The habit changes with a valid blood or a valid tuhr.

Notes

Case Fifteen

SITUATION: A woman has a 5-day menstrual habit and a 20-day tuhr habit. She has her usual 5 days of menstruation, then 14 days of tuhr, and then 5 days of blood.

HABIT

1	-	-	-	5	6	-	-	-	-	-	-	-	-	-	-	-	-	19	20	-	-	-	-	25
5 menses					20 tuhr																			

SITUATION

1	-	-	-	5	6	-	-	-	-	-	-	-	-	-	-	-	-	19	20	-	-	-	-	25
5 blood					14 tuhr														6 blood					

1. *Analysis of the Situation*
   1. The blood from day 1 to day 5 is menstruation in keeping with her habit.
   2. The tuhr from day 6 to day 19 is an invalid tuhr because it is less than 15 days and does not separate between day 5 and day 20. This tuhr is legal blood, and it is added to the blood before and after it.
   3. The blood from day 20 to day 25 is invalid because it occurs after an incomplete tuhr. It is added to the previous real and legal blood. No blood appears in the place of the habit.
   4. The total days of blood are 25.
2. *Solution*
   1. Since the blood exceeds 10 days, she returns to her menstrual habit.
   2. The menstrual habit of 5 days remains.
   3. The tuhr habit of 20 days remains.
   4. No blood occurs in the habitual place after the tuhr habit.
   5. Day 1 to day 5 is menstruation.

6. Day 6 to day 25 is istihada.

SOLUTION

1	-	-	-	5	6	-	-	-	-	-	-	-	-	-	-	-	-	19	20	-	-	-	-	25
5 menses					20 tuhr																			

3. *Rulings for the Day-by-Day Situation*

1. With the appearance of blood on day 1, it is unlawful to pray and fast.
2. When the blood stops on day 6, she is required to take a purificatory bath (ghusl), to pray, and fast if Ramadan.
3. The bleeding on day 20 makes it is clear that the previous tuhr is incomplete and the blood is istihada. She must continue praying and fasting until the days of her 20-day tuhr habit are complete, i.e. from day 20 to day 25.

4. *Precepts Applied for This Situation*

1. It is obligatory for each woman to record her menstrual, lochial, and tuhr periods.
2. Each time the blood stops before 3 days, she prays with ablution. Each time it stops after 3 days, she prays with a purificatory bath (ghusl).
3. An incomplete tuhr is considered legal blood that links the first actual bleeding to the second actual bleeding.
4. Two menstrual periods cannot succeed each other; there must be a complete tuhr interval between them.
5. The minimal tuhr interval between two menstrual periods is 15 days.

Case Sixteen

SITUATION: A woman has a 5-day menstrual habit and a 20-day tuhr habit. She has her usual 5 days of menstruation, then 14 days of tuhr, and then 9 days of blood.

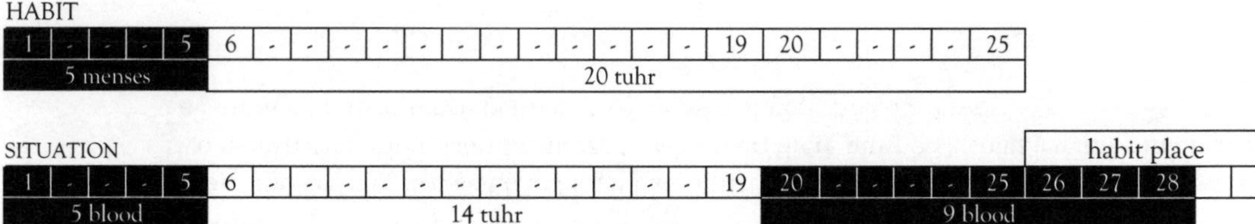

1. *Analysis of the Situation*
    1. The blood from day 1 to day 5 is menstruation in keeping with her habit.
    2. The tuhr from day 6 to day 19 is an incomplete tuhr and does not separate between the bloods before or after it; rather it links them together making the tuhr interval legal blood.
    3. The blood from day 20 to day 28 is added to the previous real and legal blood.
        a) 6 days appear in the place of the tuhr habit from day 20 to day 25.
        b) 3 days appear in the habitual place of the menstrual habit from day 26 to day 28.
    4. The total days of blood are 28.

2. *Solution*
    1. Since the blood exceeds 10 days, she returns to her habit.
        a) The place of the habit remains because the minimal amount occurred in it.
        b) The duration of the habit changes to 3 days because they occurred in the habitual place.

2. The tuhr habit of 20 days remains the same because the 14-day tuhr is invalid.
3. Day 1 to day 5 is menstruation.
4. Day 6 to day 19 is tuhr.
5. Day 20 to day 25 is istihada.
6. Day 26 to day 28 is menstruation.

SOLUTION

																									habit place		
1	-	-	-	5	6	-	-	-	-	-	-	-	-	-	-	-	-	19	20	-	-	-	-	25	26	27	28
5 menses					20 tuhr																				3 menses		

3. *Rulings for the Day-by-Day Situation*

1. With the appearance of blood on day 1, it is unlawful to pray and fast.
2. When the blood stops on day 6, she is required to take a purificatory bath (ghusl), to pray, and fast if Ramadan.
3. Upon bleeding on day 20, she continues praying and fasting from day 20 to day 25 even though she sees blood because the previous tuhr is invalid.
4. On day 26, she stops praying and fasting because this is the first day of the habitual place of her menstrual habit and there is bleeding.
5. With the cessation of blood on day 28, she is required to take a bath (ghusl), to pray, and fast.
6. On day 28, she is certain that the minimum has occurred in the habit place but the number has changed from 5 days to 3 days.

4. *Precepts Applied for This Situation*

1. It is obligatory for each woman to record her menstrual, lochial, and tuhr periods.
2. Each time the blood stops before 3 days, she prays with ablution. Each time it stops after 3 days, she prays with a purificatory bath (ghusl).
3. An incomplete tuhr is considered legal blood that links the first actual bleeding to the second actual bleeding.

4. Two menstrual periods cannot succeed each other; there must be a complete tuhr interval between them.
5. The minimal tuhr interval between two menstrual periods is 15 days.
6. If real or legal blood exceeds 10 days and a minimum in the habitual place but less than the habit, then the number changes to those that have occurred in the proper place and becomes the new habit, while the rest is istihada.
7. The habit changes with a valid blood or a valid tuhr.

14

END OF VALID BLEEDING SUMMARY

14.1

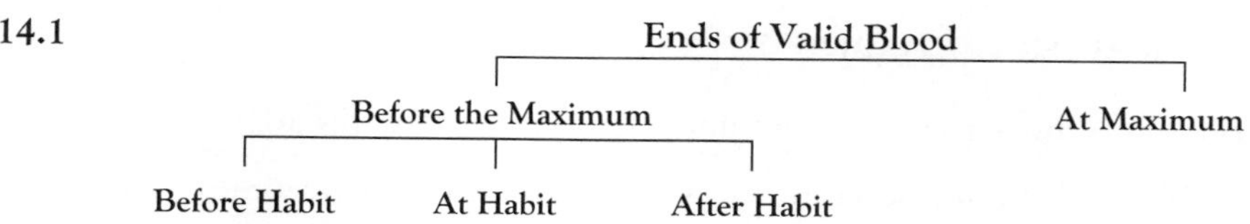

BEFORE THE HABIT

14.2 When the blood stops, one is obliged to take a purificatory bath (ghusl, def: 2.21).

14.3 If menses ends before a woman's habit, she is obliged to wait to the end of the preferred prayer time (def:2.22) to take a bath (ghusl).

14.4 The time for the bath (ghusl) is considered part of the menstrual or lochial period.

Bath (ghusl) time includes the time it takes to perform the minimal bath (ghusl), get dressed, face the direction of prayer (qibla) and say 'Allah' of 'Allahu Akbar' for the opening of the prayer.

14.5 If menses ends before a woman's habit, she is obliged to pray and fast, if Ramadan.

14.6 When a woman suspects the blood is coming to its end, she should place a kursuf properly (dis: 5.1) and check at the end of each prayer time.

'End of a prayer time' means enough time to take a bath (ghusl) and pray the prayer before its disliked time.

14.7 If the blood stops before Fajr but there is not enough time to take a bath (ghusl), then one is not obliged to perform 'Isha' prayer.

If Ramadan, one may not eat after one's bath (ghusl) and is required to act as a fasting person even though one must repeat this fast-day.

14.8 Sexual intercourse is unlawful if the bleeding stops before the habit until the completion of the habit.

In 14.20: Before the Habit this would mean in the second month she would take a bath (ghusl) on day 7, start praying and fasting, if Ramadan, but not have sexual intercourse until day 9. The following month she would take her bath (ghusl) on day 5, start her prayers and fast, if Ramadan, but not have sexual intercourse until day 7 and so forth.

AT OR AFTER THE HABIT

14.9 One is obliged to wait until all bleeding stops (dis: 6.2).

14.10 When the blood stops, one is obliged to take a purificatory bath.

14.11 If menses ends *at* or *after* a woman's habit, it is recommended, but not obligatory, to wait to the end of the preferred prayer time (def:2.22) to take a bath (ghusl).

14.12 As long as the bleeding is within the possible days of menstruation or lochia and increases but does not exceed the maximum, then her habit changes according to what she sees.

For example in 14.20: After the Habit, the first month her habit is 3 days and in the following month her habit changes to 5 days, and in the next month her habit changes again to 6 days.

14.13 The time for the bath (ghusl) is considered part of the menstrual or lochial period.

Bath (ghusl) time includes the time it takes to perform the minimal bath (ghusl), get dressed, face the direction of prayer (qibla) and say 'Allah' of 'Allahu Akbar' for the opening of the prayer.

14.14 After the purificatory bath (ghusl) sexual intercourse is permissible.

14.15 If the blood stops before Fajr (dawn) but there is not enough time to take a purificatory bath (ghusl), then one is not obliged to perform 'Isha' (nightfall) prayer.

If Ramadan, one may not eat after one's bath (ghusl) and is required to act as a fasting person even though one must repeat this fast-day.

14.16 When a woman suspects the blood is coming to its end, she should place a kursuf properly (dis: 5.1) and check at the end of each prayer time.

'End of a prayer time' means enough time to take a purificatory bath (ghusl) and pray the prayer before its disliked time.

AT THE MAXIMUM

14.17 One is obliged to take a purificatory bath (ghusl).

14.18 Sexual intercourse is permissible before the purificatory bath (ghusl) though it is disliked.

14.19 Fasting is valid if the maximum time ends before Fajr (dawn) and one makes the intention to fast; even though one does not have time to take the minimal bath (ghusl) before Fajr, there must be enough time to say 'Allah'.

In this case, one is obliged to make up 'Isha' and *witr* prayers. The bath (ghusl) is considered part of the time of tuhr.

14.20

Endings of Valid Blood

Before the Maximum for Menses

	At Habit		After Habit		Before Habit	
	Tuhr	**Blood**	**Tuhr**	**Blood**	**Tuhr**	**Blood**
Month 1		7		3		9
	21		20		20	
Month 2		7		5		7
	21		18		22	
Month 3		7		6		5
	21		17		23	

At Maximum
10 days (240 hrs)

Before the Maximum for Lochia

At Habit	After Habit	Before Habit
1st child **35** days	1st child **30** days	1st child **40** days
2nd child **35** days	2nd child **33** days	2nd child **32** days
3rd child **35** days	3rd child **39** days	3rd child **25** days

At Maximum
40 days (960 hrs)

15

Abnormal Vaginal Discharge

The following general information has been taken from the *Harvard Guide to Women's Health*, *Merck Manual of Medical Information (Home Edition)*, and *Women's Bodies, Women's Wisdom*.

15.1 Normally all women produce a slight vaginal discharge, which varies in amount and quality depending on the time of the month.

15.2 This discharge is odorless, non-irritating, and can be clear, milky, whitish, or sometimes clumpy.

15.3 It typically increases as ovulation approaches, when it becomes thin and clear, like raw egg white.

15.4 Discharge typically increases during pregnancy, sexual arousal [madhy] and stress, or after birth-control pills have been discontinued.

15.5 Often, an abnormal discharge is thicker than a normal discharge and varies in color. For example, it may be the consistency of cottage cheese, or it may be yellow, greenish, or blood-tinged.

Types of Abnormal Vaginal Discharge

15.6 A discharge is considered abnormal if it occurs in large amounts, has an offensive odor, or is accompanied by vaginal itching, soreness, or pain.

1. The vagina and vulva burn, itch, or swell.
2. There may be pain during urination, but unlike the internal burning felt during a urinary tract infection, the urinary pain associated with vaginitis is usually sharp and external because it results from urine hitting the irritated vaginal lips.
3. There may be pain during sexual intercourse.

15.7 When the vaginal defenses are down, the way is cleared for various infections.

15.8 Women can have more than one type of vaginal infection at a time.

15.9 Vaginitis literally means inflammation of the vagina in which there is an abnormal vaginal discharge accompanied by vaginal irritation.

Vaginitis is a common and often frustrating problem that can occur whenever the normal balance of organisms that live in the vagina are upset.

15.10 The vagina is acidic with a pH 3.8 to 4.2 and is inhospitable to disease-causing bacteria, fungi, and protozoa.

15.11 The discharge that occurs in vaginitis, in contrast to normal vaginal discharge, appears gray, greenish, frothy, cheesy, smelly, or particularly profuse.

15.12 A bacterial infection of the vagina tends to produce a white, gray, or yellowish cloudy discharge with a foul or fishy odor.

1. The odor may become stronger after sexual intercourse or washing with soap, both of which reduce vaginal acidity, thus encouraging bacterial growth.
2. The vulva may feel irritated or itch mildly.

15.13 A candidal (yeast) infection produces moderate to severe itching and burning of the vulva and vagina.

1. The skin appears red and may feel raw.
2. A thick cheesy discharge from the vagina tends to cling to the vaginal wall.
3. Symptoms may worsen during the week before a menstrual period.
4. This infection tends to recur in women who have diabetes that is not well-controlled and in those who are taking antibiotics.

15.14 An infection by Trichomonas vaginalis, a protozoan, produces a white, grayish-green, or yellowish discharge that may be frothy.

1. The discharge often appears shortly after a menstrual period and may have an unpleasant odor.
2. Itching is severe.

15.15 Vulvitis is an inflammation of the vulva.

15.16 A painful sore on the vulva may be caused by a herpes infection or an abscess.

15.17 A sore that is not painful may be caused by syphilis.

15.18 Pubic lice and scabies cause itching in the area of the vulva.

CAUSES OF ABNORMAL VAGINAL DISCHARGE

15.19 Among the many factors that can alter the vaginal environment are antibiotics taken to treat another infection, birth-control pills, estrogen replacement therapy, douching, diabetes, and pregnancy.

15.20 Lack of sleep, inadequate diet, poor hygiene, and stress may also lower a woman's resistance to vaginitis.

15.21 Having sexual intercourse with a spouse infected with a sexually transmitted disease is a risk factor as well.

15.22 All women should avoid using pads and tampons that contain deodorants.

1. These tampons can produce vaginal ulcers, and the pads can cause vulvar irritation.
2. No tampon should ever be left inside the vagina for more than four to eight hours at a time (dis: 15.37-42 below).

15.23 Other irritants can include chemicals in swimming pools and hot tubs, scented douches, and vulvar deodorants.

15.24 Repeated intercourse in a short period of time where the husband ejaculates inside the vagina can increase the pH of the vagina because semen is a buffered alkaline fluid, with a pH of about 9.

1. When vaginal pH is higher than normal for long periods of time, the bacterial balance can be lost. Those organisms that are normally present only in small numbers can begin to grow and cause infection-like symptoms.
2. If a woman has sexual intercourse with ejaculation of semen into the vagina three times in a 24-hour period, her vagina will not return to its normal pH for that entire 24-hour period. For some women, this is a set-up for infection, particularly women who are in long-distance relationships and whose sex lives are sporadic and limited to increased activity over a few days.
3. While douching is generally not recommended, in this situation it is helpful to prevent problems. One can douche

within a few hours of intercourse with a medicated douche, which contains potassium iodide and lowers vaginal pH. Or use a vinegar douche—one tablespoon per quart of warm water.

PREVENTING VAGINITIS AND VULVITIS

15.25 Some basic health and hygiene practices may help prevent both vaginal infections and vulvitis.

1. Getting enough rest, eating a nutritious diet, and finding ways to cope with stress can increase resistance to vaginal infections.
2. Keeping the vulva as clean, dry, and cool as possible can prevent the overgrowth of harmful microorganisms.
3. Wiping from front to back after a bowel movement so that bacteria from the gastrointestinal tract does not spread into the vaginal area.

15.26 For vaginal infections the standard treatment is a specific medication, which kills the responsible microorganism. Sometimes the spouse may need to take the drug as well.

15.27 Some women develop vulvar irritation through chemical irritants found in scented, softened, and colored toilet paper, bubble baths, and sanitary tampons and pads that contain deodorants.

15.28 Douching can actually predispose a woman to vaginal infections by changing the acidity of the vagina and encouraging the growth of potentially harmful microorganisms. (Dis: 15.24 for an exception.)

15.29 Similarly, tampons and sanitary napkins that contain deodorants and feminine hygiene sprays may do more harm than good by killing some of the protective lactobacilli.

15.30 Many women prone to vaginitis and vulvitis advocate avoiding synthetic undergarments and tight jeans probably because these increase heat and moisture and therefore foster bacterial growth.

15.31 Spermicides—jellies, creams, or foams—themselves can sometimes cause vaginal irritation.

15.32 If sexual intercourse is painful, using a water-soluble lubricant, such as Astroglide, can help prevent unnecessary irritation to the vaginal tissues.

15.33 If vaginal atrophy is a problem, using a water-soluble lubricant can help prevent unnecessary irritation to the vaginal tissues.

15.34 If you have tried an over-the-counter preparation for a week or so with no improvement of your symptoms, see a health-care practitioner.

15.35 Once a diagnosis of a vaginal infection is made, the practitioner can prescribe the proper treatment.

15.36 Evidence also suggests that some women have chronic yeast infections even after treatment because they are continually re-infected by their husbands. In these cases, treatment of the husband is helpful, if not essential.

TOXIC SHOCK SYNDROME

15.37 Toxic Shock Syndrome (TSS) is an acute infection characterized by high fever, a sunburn-like rash, vomiting and diarrhea, followed in severe cases by shock.

15.38 TSS is usually caused by a toxin-producing strain of the staphylococci aureus. Although this strain is known, the event that triggers the syndrome is not.

15.39 The presence of a tampon may encourage the bacteria to produce a toxin that enters the blood through small cuts in the vaginal lining or through the uterus into the abdominal cavity.

15.40 TSS most frequently occurs among menstruating women who use vaginal tampons.

15.41 Studies have concluded that high-absorbency tampons increase the risk of TSS.

15.42 Most companies recommend:

1. changing tampons every 4 to 8 hours during the day;
2. not using tampons between periods or for non-menstrual discharge.

Common Types of Vaginitis

Conditions	Symptoms	Amount of Discharge	Appearance of Discharge	Odor of Discharge
Normal vagina	None	Usually 4-5 cc per day but increases around time of ovulation and during pregnancy; decreases after menopause	Clear or white	None
Bacterial vaginosis	None or irritation	Increases	Homogeneous, gray	Fishy, especially after intercourse or washing with soap
Yeast infection	Itching, burning	Usually increases	Cottage cheesy, white	Sweet or bread-like
Trichomonas	Itching	Increases	Frothy, green, or gray	Foul
Atrophic vaginitis (vaginal atrophy)	Irritation, itching, pain during sexual intercourse	None or increases	Watery, yellow, or green	None
Cytologic vaginosis	Burning, itching, irritation, pain during sexual intercourse; symptoms may worsen during second half of menstrual cycle	Increases	Clumpy, white	None
Retained foreign bodies (tampons, diaphragms)	None or discharge	Profuse	Watery or bloody	Foul

(Carlson et al., 1996. p. 631)

Appendix 1: The Arabic Text

ذخر المتأهلين والنساء في تعريف الأطهار والدماء

للإمام محمد پير علي البرگوي

929 - 981 هـ

بسم الله الرحمن الرحيم

الْحَمْدُ لله الَّذِي جَعَلَ الرِّجَالَ عَلَى النِّسَاءِ قَوَّامِينَ، وَأَمَرَهُمْ بِوَعْظِهِنَّ وَالتَّأْدِيبِ وَتَعْلِيمِ الدِّينِ. وَالصَّلاةُ وَالسَّلامُ عَلَى حَبِيبِ رَبِّ الْعَالَمِينَ، وَعَلَى آلِهِ وَأَصْحَابِهِ هُدَاةِ الْحَقِّ وَحُمَاةِ الشَّرْعِ المَتِينِ.

وَبَعْدُ: فَقَدِ اتَّفَقَ الْفُقَهَاءُ عَلَى فَرْضِيَّةِ عِلْمِ الْحَالِ عَلَى كُلِّ مَنْ آمَنَ بِالله وَالْيَوْمِ الآخِرِ مِنْ نِسْوَةٍ وَرِجَالٍ. فَمَعْرِفَةُ الدِّمَاءِ الْمُخْتَصَّةِ بِالنِّسَاءِ وَاجِبَةٌ عَلَيْهِنَّ وَعَلَى الأَزْوَاجِ وَالأَوْلِيَاءِ، وَلَكِنَّ هَذَا كَانَ فِي زَمَانِنَا مَهْجُوراً، بَلْ صَارَ كَأَنْ لَمْ يَكُنْ شَيْئاً مَذْكُوراً. لا يُفَرِّقُونَ بَيْنَ الْحَيْضِ وَالنِّفَاسِ وَالاسْتِحَاضَةِ، وَلا يُمَيِّزُونَ بَيْنَ الصَّحِيحَةِ - مِنَ الدِّمَاءِ وَالأَطْهَارِ- وَالْفَاسِدَةِ. تَرَى أَمْثَلَهُمْ يَكْتَفِي بِالْمُتُونِ الْمَشْهُورَةِ، وَأَكْثَرُ مَسَائِلِ الدِّمَاءِ فِيهَا مَفْقُودَةٌ.

وَالْكُتُبُ الْمَبْسُوطَةُ لا يَمْلِكُهَا إِلَّا قَلِيلٌ. وَالْمَالِكُونَ أَكْثَرُهُمْ عَنْ مُطَالَعَتِهَا عَاجِزٌ وَعَلِيلٌ. وَأَكْثَرُ نُسَخِهَا فِي بَابِ حَيْضِهَا تَحْرِيفٌ وَتَبْدِيلٌ ؛ لِعَدَمِ الاشْتِغَالِ بِهِ مُنْذُ دَهْرٍ طَوِيلٍ. وَفِي مَسَائِلِهِ كَثْرَةٌ وَصُعُوبَةٌ وَاخْتِلافَاتٌ. وَفِي اخْتِيَارِ الْمَشَايِخِ وَتَصْحِيحِهِمْ أَيْضاً مُخَالَفَاتٌ.

فَأَرَدْتُ أَنْ أُصَنِّفَ رِسَالَةً حَاوِيَةً لِمَسَائِلِهِ اللازِمَةِ، خَاوِيَةً عَنْ ذِكْرِ خِلافٍ وَمَبَاحِثَ غَيْرِ مُهِمَّةٍ، مُقْتَصِرَةً عَلَى الأَقْوَى وَالأَصَحِّ وَالْمُخْتَارِ لِلْفَتْوَى، مُسَهِّلَةً الضَّبْطَ وَالْفَهْمَ. رَجَاءَ أَنْ تَكُونَ لِي ذُخْراً فِي الْعُقْبَى.

فَيَا أَيُّهَا النَّاظِرُ إِلَيْهَا - بِالله الْعَظِيمِ - لا تَعْجَلْ فِي التَّخْطِئَةِ بِمُجَرَّدِ رُؤْيَتِكَ فِيهَا الْمُخَالَفَةَ لِظَاهِرِ بَعْضِ الْكُتُبِ الْمَشْهُورَةِ. فَعَسَى أَنْ تُخَطِّئَ ابْنَ أُخْتِ خَالَتِكَ فَتَكُونَ مِنَ الَّذِينَ هَلَكُوا فِي الْمَهَالِكِ. فَإِنِّي قَدْ صَرَفْتُ شَطْراً مِنْ عُمْرِي فِي ضَبْطِ هَذَا الْبَابِ حَتَّى مَيَّزْتُ -بِفَضْلِ الله تَعَالَى- بَيْنَ الْقِشْرِ وَاللُّبَابِ، وَالسَّمِينِ وَالْمَهْزُولِ، وَالصَّحِيحِ وَالْمَعْلُولِ، وَالْجَيِّدِ وَالرَّدِيءِ، وَالضَّعِيفِ

وَالقَوِيِّ. وَرَجَّحْتُ بِأَسْبَابِ التَّرْجِيحِ المُعْتَبَرَةِ مَا هُوَ الرَّاجِحُ مِنَ الأَقْوَالِ وَالاخْتِيَارَاتِ مِنَ الأَئِمَّةِ.

فَارْجِعِ البَصَرَ كَرَّتَيْنِ، وَتَأَمَّلْ مَا كَتَبْنَا مَرَّتَيْنِ، وَاعْرِضْهُ عَلَى الفُرُوعِ وَالأُصُولِ وَقَوَاعِدِ المَنْقُولِ وَالمَعْقُولِ، لَعَلَّكَ تَطَّلِعُ عَلَى حَقِّيَّتِهِ، وَتَظْهَرُ لَكَ وُجُوهُ صِحَّتِهِ، وَتَرْجِعُ إِلَى التَّصْوِيبِ مِنْ تَخْطِئَتِهِ، وَتَقُولُ: ﴿ الحمدُ لله الَّذِي هَدَانَا لِهَذَا وَمَا كُنَّا لِنَهْتَدِيَ لَوْلَا أَنْ هَدَانَا اللهُ﴾.

فَنَقُولُ – وَبِاللهِ التَّوْفِيقُ وَمِنْهُ كُلُّ تَحْقِيقٍ وَتَدْقِيقٍ – هَذِهِ الرِّسَالَةُ مُرَتَّبَةٌ عَلَى مُقَدِّمَةٍ وَفُصُولٍ.

أَمَّا المُقَدِّمَةُ فَفِيهَا نَوْعَانِ:

النَّوْعُ الأَوَّلُ: فِي تَفْسِيرِ الأَلْفَاظِ المُسْتَعْمَلَةِ.

اعْلَمْ أَنَّ الدِّمَاءَ المُخْتَصَّةَ بِالنِّسَاءِ ثَلَاثَةٌ: حَيْضٌ، وَنِفَاسٌ، وَاسْتِحَاضَةٌ.

فَالحَيْضُ: دَمٌ صَادِرٌ مِنْ رَحِمٍ، خَارِجٌ مِنْ فَرْجٍ دَاخِلٍ، وَلَوْ حُكْماً، بِدُونِ وِلَادَةٍ.

وَالنِّفَاسُ: دَمٌ كَذَلِكَ عَقِيبَ خُرُوجِ أَكْثَرِ وَلَدٍ، لَمْ يَسْبِقْهُ وَلَدٌ مُذْ أَقَلَّ مِنْ سِتَّةِ أَشْهُرٍ.

وَالاسْتِحَاضَةُ: وَيُسَمَّى دَماً فَاسِداً: دَمٌ–وَلَوْ حُكْماً–خَارِجٌ مِنْ فَرْجٍ دَاخِلٍ، لَا عَنْ رَحِمٍ.

وَالدَّمُ الصَّحِيحُ: مَا لَا يَنْقُصُ عَنْ ثَلَاثَةٍ وَلَا يَزِيدُ عَلَى العَشَرَةِ فِي الحَيْضِ، وَلَا عَلَى الأَرْبَعِينَ فِي النِّفَاسِ، وَلَا يَكُونُ فِي أَحَدِ طَرَفَيْهِ دَمٌ وَلَوْ حُكْماً.

وَالطُّهْرُ المُطْلَقُ: مَا لَا يَكُونُ حَيْضاً، وَلَا نِفَاساً.

وَالطُّهْرُ الصَّحِيحُ: مَا لَا يَكُونُ أَقَلَّ مِنْ خَمْسَةَ عَشَرَ يَوْماً، وَلَا يَشُوبُهُ دَمٌ، وَيَكُونُ بَيْنَ الدَّمَيْنِ الصَّحِيحَيْنِ.

وَالطُّهْرُ الفَاسِدُ: مَا خَالَفَهُ فِي وَاحِدٍ مِنْهُ، وَالطُّهْرُ المُتَخَلِّلُ مُطْلَقاً بَيْنَ الأَرْبَعِينَ فِي النِّفَاسِ.

وَالطُّهْرُ التَّامُّ: طُهْرٌ خَمْسَةَ عَشَرَ يَوْماً فَصَاعِداً.

وَالطُّهْرُ النَّاقِصُ: مَا نَقَصَ مِنْهُ.

وَالمُعْتَادَةُ: مَنْ سَبَقَ مِنْهَا دَمٌ وَطُهْرٌ صَحِيحَانِ، أَوْ أَحَدُهُمَا.

وَالمُبْتَدَأَةُ: مَنْ كَانَتْ فِي أَوَّلِ حَيْضٍ أَوْ نِفَاسٍ.

وَالمُضِلَّةُ: وَتُسَمَّى الضَّالَّةَ وَالمُتَحَيِّرَةَ: مَنْ نَسِيَتْ عَادَتَهَا فِي حَيْضٍ أَوْ نِفَاسٍ.

النَّوْعُ الثَّانِي: فِي الأُصُولِ وَالْقَوَاعِدِ الْكُلِّيَّةِ.

أَقَلُّ الحَيْضِ: ثَلاثَةُ أَيَّامٍ وَلَيَالِيهَا، أَعْنِي: اثْنَتَيْنِ وَسَبْعِينَ سَاعَةً. حَتَّى لَوْ رَأَتْ مَثَلاً عِنْدَ طُلُوعِ شَمْسِ يَوْمِ الأَحَدِ سَاعَةً، ثُمَّ انْقَطَعَ إِلَى فَجْرِ يَوْمِ الأَرْبِعَاءِ، ثُمَّ رَأَتْ قُبَيْلَ طُلُوعِهَا، ثُمَّ انْقَطَعَ عِنْدَ الطُّلُوعِ، أَوِ اسْتَمَرَّ مِنَ الطُّلُوعِ الأَوَّلِ إِلَى الثَّانِي يَكُونُ حَيْضاً. وَلَوِ انْقَطَعَ قَبْلَ الطُّلُوعِ الثَّانِي بِزَمَانٍ يَسِيرٍ وَلَمْ يَتَّصِلْ بِهِ الدَّمُ، ثُمَّ لَمْ تَرَ دَماً إِلَى تَمَامِ خَمْسَةَ عَشَرَ يَوْماً لَمْ يَكُنْ حَيْضاً. وَأَكْثَرُهُ: عَشَرَةٌ كَذَلِكَ.

وَأَقَلُّ النِّفَاسِ: لا حَدَّ لَهُ. حَتَّى إِذَا وَلَدَتْ فَانْقَطَعَ الدَّمُ تَغْتَسِلُ وَتُصَلِّي. وَأَكْثَرُهُ: أَرْبَعُونَ يَوْماً.

فَالحَيْضَانِ لا يَتَوَالَيَانِ، وَكَذَا النِّفَاسَانِ، وَالنِّفَاسُ وَالحَيْضُ، بَلْ لابُدَّ مِنْ طُهْرٍ بَيْنَهُمَا.

وَأَقَلُّ الطُّهْرِ: فِي حَقِّ النِّفَاسَيْنِ سِتَّةُ أَشْهُرٍ، وَفِي غَيْرِهِمَا خَمْسَةَ عَشَرَ يَوْماً. فَالدَّمَانِ المُحِيطَانِ بِهِ حَيْضَانِ إِنْ بَلَغَ كُلٌّ نِصَاباً، وَلَمْ يَمْنَعْ مَانِعٌ، وَإِلَّا فَاسْتِحَاضَةٌ أَوْ نِفَاسٌ. وَالطُّهْرُ النَّاقِصُ كَالدَّمِ المُتَوَالِي لا يَفْصِلُ بَيْنَ الدَّمَيْنِ مُطْلَقاً. وَكَذَا الطُّهْرُ الْفَاسِدُ فِي النِّفَاسِ. وَأَكْثَرُ الطُّهْرِ: لا حَدَّ لَهُ إِلَّا عِنْدَ نَصْبِ الْعَادَةِ. وَسَيَجِيءُ إِنْ شَاءَ اللهُ تَعَالَى.

وَالْعَادَةُ تَثْبُتُ بِمَرَّةٍ وَاحِدَةٍ فِي الحَيْضِ وَالنِّفَاسِ، دَماً أَوْ طُهْراً، إِنْ كَانَا صَحِيحَيْنِ.

وَتَنْتَقِلُ كَذَلِكَ:

- زَمَاناً: بِأَنْ لَمْ تَرَ فِيهِ، أَوْ رَأَتْ قَبْلَهُ.

- وَعَدَداً: إِنْ رَأَتْ مَا يُخَالِفُهُ صَحِيحاً - طُهْراً أَوْ دَماً - أَوْ دَماً فَاسِداً جَاوَزَ الْعَشَرَةَ وَوَقَعَ نِصَابٌ فِي بَعْضِ الْعَادَةِ وَبَعْضُهَا مِنَ الطُّهْرِ الصَّحِيحِ.

أَمَّا الْفُصُولُ فَسِتَّةٌ:

الْفَصْلُ الأَوَّلُ: فِي ابْتِدَاءِ ثُبُوتِ الدِّمَاءِ الثَّلاثَةِ، وَانْتِهَائِهِ، وَالْكُرْسُفِ.

أَمَّا الأَوَّلُ: فَعِنْدَ ظُهُورِ الدَّمِ ؛ بِأَنْ خَرَجَ مِنَ الْفَرْجِ الدَّاخِلِ أَوْ حَاذَى حَرْفَهُ، كَالْبَوْلِ وَالْغَائِطِ. فَكُلُّ مَا ظَهَرَ مِنَ الإِحْلِيلِ وَالدُّبُرِ وَالْفَرْجِ بِأَنْ سَاوَى الحَرْفَ يَنْتَقِضُ بِهِ الْوُضُوءُ مُطْلَقاً، وَيَثْبُتُ بِهِ النِّفَاسُ وَالحَيْضُ إِنْ كَانَ دَماً صَحِيحاً مِنْ بِنْتِ تِسْعِ سِنِينَ أَوْ أَكْثَرَ.

فَإِنْ أُحِسَّ ابْتِدَاءَ بِنُزُولِهِ وَلَمْ يَظْهَرْ، أَوْ مُنِعَ مِنْهُ بِالشَّدِّ أَوْ الاحْتِشَاءِ فَلَيْسَ لَهُ حُكْمٌ. وَإِنْ مُنِعَ

بَعْدَ الظُّهُورِ أَوَّلاً فَالْحَيْضُ وَالنِّفَاسُ بَاقِيَانِ دُونَ الاسْتِحَاضَةِ.

وَأَمَّا فِي غَيْرِ السَّبِيلَيْنِ فَلا حُكْمَ لِلظُّهُورِ وَالْمُحَاذَاةِ، بَلْ لابُدَّ مِنَ الْخُرُوجِ وَالسَّيَلانِ - إِلَى مَا يَجِبُ تَطْهِيرُهُ فِي الْغُسْلِ- فِي نَقْضِ الْوُضُوءِ. فَلَوْ مُنِعَ الْجُرْحُ السَّائِلُ مِنَ السَّيَلانِ انْتَفَى الْعُذْرُ بِلا خِلافٍ، كَالاسْتِحَاضَةِ.

وَفِي النِّفَاسِ لابُدَّ مَعَ ذَلِكَ مِنْ خُرُوجِ أَكْثَرِ الْوَلَدِ. فَإِنْ وَلَدَتْ وَلَمْ تَرَ دَماً فَعَلَيْهَا الْغُسْلُ؛ لأَنَّ الْوَلَدَ لا يَنْفَكُّ عَنْ بِلَّةِ دَمٍ. وَلَوْ خَرَجَ الْوَلَدُ مِنْ غَيْرِ الْفَرْجِ، إِنْ خَرَجَ الدَّمُ مِنَ الْفَرْجِ فَنِفَاسٌ، وَإِلَّا فَلا.

وَالسِّقْطُ إِنِ اسْتَبَانَ بَعْضُ خَلْقِهِ كَالشَّعْرِ وَالظُّفْرِ فَوَلَدٌ، وَإِلَّا فَلا. وَلَكِنَّ مَا رَأَتْهُ مِنَ الدَّمِ حَيْضٌ إِنْ بَلَغَ نِصَاباً وَتَقَدَّمَهُ طُهْرٌ تَامٌ، وَإِلَّا فَاسْتِحَاضَةٌ.

وَإِنْ وَلَدَتْ وَلَدَيْنِ أَوْ أَكْثَرَ فِي بَطْنٍ وَاحِدٍ: بِأَنْ كَانَ بَيْنَ كُلِّ وَلَدَيْنِ أَقَلُّ مِنْ سِتَّةِ أَشْهُرٍ، فَالنِّفَاسُ مِنَ الأَوَّلِ فَقَطْ.

وَأَمَّا انْتِهَاءُ الْحَيْضِ: فَبِبُلُوغِهَا سِنَّ الإِيَاسِ. وَهُوَ فِي الْحَيْضِ خَمْسٌ وَخَمْسُونَ سَنَةً. فَإِنْ رَأَتْ بَعْدَهُ دَماً خَالِصاً نِصَاباً فَحَيْضٌ، وَإِلَّا فَاسْتِحَاضَةٌ.

وَفِي غَيْرِ الآيِسَةِ مَا عَدَا الْبَيَاضَ الْخَالِصَ مِنَ الأَلْوَانِ فِي حُكْمِ الدَّمِ. وَالْمُعْتَبَرُ فِي اللَّوْنِ حِينَ يَرْتَفِعُ الْحَشْوُ وَهُوَ طَرِيٌّ، وَلا يُعْتَبَرُ التَّغَيُّرُ بَعْدَ ذَلِكَ.

وَأَمَّا الْكُرْسُفُ: فَسُنَّةٌ لِلْبِكْرِ عِنْدَ الْحَيْضِ فَقَطْ، وَلِلثَّيِّبِ مُطْلَقاً. وَيُسَنُّ تَطْيِيبُهُ بِمِسْكٍ وَنَحْوِهِ. وَيُكْرَهُ وَضْعُهُ فِي الْفَرْجِ الدَّاخِلِ.

وَلَوْ وَضَعَتِ الْكُرْسُفَ فِي اللَّيْلِ مَثَلاً وَهِيَ حَائِضَةٌ أَوْ نُفَسَاءُ، فَنَظَرَتْ فِي الصَّبَاحِ فَرَأَتْ عَلَيْهِ الْبَيَاضَ حُكِمَ بِطَهَارَتِهَا مِنْ حِينَ وَضَعَتْ، فَعَلَيْهَا قَضَاءُ الْعِشَاءِ. وَلَوْ طَاهِرَةً فَرَأَتْ عَلَيْهِ الدَّمَ فَحَيْضٌ مِنْ حِينَ رَأَتْ.

ثُمَّ إِنَّ الْكُرْسُفَ إِمَّا أَنْ يُوضَعَ فِي الْفَرْجِ الْخَارِجِ أَوِ الدَّاخِلِ. وَفِي الأَوَّلِ: إِنِ ابْتَلَّ شَيْءٌ مِنْهُ يَثْبُتُ الْحَيْضُ وَنَقْضُ الْوُضُوءِ. وَفِي الثَّانِي: إِنِ ابْتَلَّ الْجَانِبُ الدَّاخِلُ وَلَمْ تَنْفُذِ الْبِلَّةُ إِلَى مَا يُحَاذِي حَرْفَ الْفَرْجِ الدَّاخِلِ لا يَثْبُتُ شَيْءٌ، إِلَّا أَنْ يَخْرُجَ الْكُرْسُفُ. وَإِنْ نَفَذَ فَيَثْبُتُ. وَإِنْ كَانَ الْكُرْسُفُ كُلُّهُ فِي الدَّاخِلِ فَابْتَلَّ كُلُّهُ، فَإِنْ كَانَ مُتَسَفِّلاً عَنْ حَرْفِ الدَّاخِلِ فَلا حُكْمَ لَهُ، وَإِلَّا فَخُرُوجٌ. وَكَذَا

الْحُكْمُ فِي الذِّكْرِ. وَكُلُّ هَذَا مَفْهُومٌ مِمَّا سَبَقَ، وَتَفْصِيلٌ لَهُ.

الْفَصْلُ الثَّانِي: فِي الْمُبْتَدَأَةِ وَالْمُعْتَادَةِ.

أَمَّا الأُولَى: فَكُلُّ مَا رَأَتْ حَيْضٌ وَنِفَاسٌ، إِلَّا مَا جَاوَزَ أَكْثَرَهُمَا. وَلا تَنْسَ كَوْنَ الطُّهْرِ النَّاقِصِ كَالْمُتَوَالِي. فَإِنْ رَأَتِ سَاعَةً دَماً ثُمَّ أَرْبَعَةَ عَشَرَ يَوْماً طُهْراً ثُمَّ سَاعَةً دَماً، فَالْعَشَرَةُ مِنْ أَوَّلِهِ حَيْضٌ، فَتَغْتَسِلُ وَتَقْضِي صَوْمَهَا. فَيَجُوزُ خَتْمُ حَيْضِهَا بِالطُّهْرِ لا بَدْؤُهَا. وَلَوْ وَلَدَتْ فَانْقَطَعَ دَمُهَا، ثُمَّ رَأَتْ آخِرَ الأَرْبَعِينَ دَماً فَكُلُّهُ نِفَاسٌ. وَإِنِ انْقَطَعَ فِي آخِرِ ثَلاثِينَ، ثُمَّ عَادَ قَبْلَ تَمَامِ خَمْسٍ وَأَرْبَعِينَ فَالأَرْبَعُونَ نِفَاسٌ. وَإِنْ عَادَ بَعْدَ تَمَامِ خَمْسٍ وَأَرْبَعِينَ فَالنِّفَاسُ ثَلاثُونَ فَقَطْ.

وَأَمَّا الْمُعْتَادَةُ: فَإِنْ رَأَتْ مَا يُوَافِقُهَا فَظَاهِرٌ. وَإِنْ رَأَتْ مَا يُخَالِفُهَا فَتَتَوَقَّفُ مَعْرِفَتُهُ عَلَى انْتِقَالِ الْعَادَةِ. فَإِنْ لَمْ تَنْتَقِلْ رُدَّتْ إِلَى عَادَتِهَا وَالْبَاقِي اِسْتِحَاضَةٌ، وَإِلَّا فَالْكُلُّ حَيْضٌ أَوْ نِفَاسٌ.

وَقَدْ عَرَفْتَ فِي الْمُقَدِّمَةِ قَاعِدَةَ الانْتِقَالِ إِجْمَالاً، وَلَكِنْ نُفَصِّلُ هَهُنَا تَسْهِيلاً لِلْمُبْتَدِئِينَ. فَنَقُولُ وَبِاللهِ التَّوْفِيقُ: الْمُخَالَفَةُ:

- إِنْ كَانَتْ فِي النِّفَاسِ، فَإِنْ جَاوَزَ الدَّمُ الأَرْبَعِينَ فَالْعَادَةُ بَاقِيَةٌ رُدَّتْ إِلَيْهَا، وَالْبَاقِي اِسْتِحَاضَةٌ. وَإِنْ لَمْ يُجَاوِزِ انْتَقَلَتْ إِلَى مَا رَأَتْهُ، فَالْكُلُّ نِفَاسٌ.

- وَإِنْ كَانَتْ فِي الْحَيْضِ، فَإِنْ جَاوَزَ الدَّمُ الْعَشَرَةَ، فَإِنْ لَمْ يَقَعْ فِي زَمَانِهَا نِصَابٌ انْتَقَلَتْ زَمَاناً، وَالْعَدَدُ بِحَالِهِ يُعْتَبَرُ مِنْ أَوَّلِ مَا رَأَتْ. وَإِنْ وَقَعَ فَالْوَاقِعُ فِي زَمَانِهَا فَقَطْ حَيْضٌ، وَالْبَاقِي اسْتِحَاضَةٌ. فَإِنْ كَانَ الْوَاقِعُ مُسَاوِياً لِعَادَتِهَا عَدَداً فَالْعَادَةُ بَاقِيَةٌ، وَإِلَّا انْتَقَلَتْ عَدَداً إِلَى مَا رَأَتْهُ نَاقِصاً، وَإِنْ لَمْ يُجَاوِزْ فَالْكُلُّ حَيْضٌ. فَإِنْ لَمْ يَتَسَاوَيَا عَدَداً صَارَ الثَّانِي عَادَةً، وَإِلَّا فَالْعَدَدُ بِحَالِهِ. وَلْنُمَثِّلْ بِأَمْثِلَةٍ تَوْضِيحاً لِلطَّالِبِينَ.

أَمْثِلَةُ النِّفَاسِ

امْرَأَةٌ عَادَتُهَا فِي النِّفَاسِ عِشْرُونَ وَلَدَتْ:

- فَرَأَتْ عَشَرَةً دَماً، وَعِشْرِينَ طُهْراً، وَأَحَدَ عَشَرَ دَماً.
- أَوْ رَأَتْ يَوْماً دَماً، وَثَلاثِينَ طُهْراً، وَيَوْماً دَماً، وَأَرْبَعَةَ عَشَرَ طُهْراً، وَيَوْماً دَماً.
- أَوْ رَأَتْ خَمْسَةً دَماً، وَأَرْبَعَةً وَثَلاثِينَ طُهْراً، وَيَوْماً دَماً.

– أَوْ رَأَتْ ثَمَانِيَةَ عَشَرَ دَماً، وَاثْنَيْنِ وَعِشْرِينَ طُهْراً، وَيَوْماً دَماً.

– أَوْ رَأَتْ يَوْماً دَماً، وَأَرْبَعَةً وَثَلَاثِينَ طُهْراً، وَيَوْماً دَماً، وَخَمْسَةَ عَشَرَ طُهْراً، وَيَوْماً دَماً.

وَأَمْثِلَةُ الْحَيْضِ

امْرَأَةٌ عَادَتُهَا فِي الْحَيْضِ خَمْسَةٌ وَطُهْرُهَا خَمْسَةٌ وَخَمْسُونَ:

– رَأَتْ عَلَى عَادَتِهَا فِي الْحَيْضِ خَمْسَةً دَماً، وَخَمْسَةَ عَشَرَ طُهْراً، وَأَحَدَ عَشَرَ دَماً.

– أَوْ رَأَتْ خَمْسَةً دَماً، وَسِتَّةً وَأَرْبَعِينَ طُهْراً، وَأَحَدَ عَشَرَ دَماً.

– أَوْ رَأَتْ خَمْسَةً دَماً، وَثَمَانِيَةً وَأَرْبَعِينَ طُهْراً، وَاثْنَيْ عَشَرَ دَماً.

– أَوْ رَأَتْ خَمْسَةً دَماً، وَأَرْبَعَةً وَخَمْسِينَ طُهْراً، وَيَوْماً دَماً، وَأَرْبَعَةَ عَشَرَ طُهْراً، وَيَوْماً دَماً.

– أَوْ رَأَتْ خَمْسَةً دَماً، وَسَبْعَةً وَخَمْسِينَ طُهْراً، وَثَلَاثَةً دَماً، وَأَرْبَعَةَ عَشَرَ طُهْراً، وَيَوْماً دَماً.

– أَوْ رَأَتْ خَمْسَةً دَماً، وَخَمْسَةً وَخَمْسِينَ طُهْراً، وَتِسْعَةً دَماً.

– أَوْ رَأَتْ خَمْسَةً دَماً، وَخَمْسِينَ طُهْراً، وَعَشَرَةً دَماً.

– أَوْ رَأَتْ خَمْسَةً دَماً، وَأَرْبَعَةً وَخَمْسِينَ طُهْراً، وَثَمَانِيَةً دَماً.

– أَوْ رَأَتْ خَمْسَةً دَماً، وَخَمْسِينَ طُهْراً، وَسَبْعَةً دَماً.

– أَوْ رَأَتْ خَمْسَةً دَماً، وَثَمَانِيَةً وَخَمْسِينَ طُهْراً، وَثَلَاثَةً دَماً.

– أَوْ رَأَتْ خَمْسَةً دَماً، وَأَرْبَعَةً وَسِتِّينَ طُهْراً، وَسَبْعَةً أَوْ أَحَدَ عَشَرَ دَماً.

فَيَجُوزُ بَدْءُ الْمُعْتَادَةِ وَخَتْمُهَا بِالطُّهْرِ.

الْفَصْلَ الثَّالِثُ: فِي الِانْقِطَاعِ.

إِنِ انْقَطَعَ الدَّمُ عَلَى أَكْثَرِ الْمُدَّةِ فِي الْحَيْضِ وَفِي النَّفَاسِ يُحْكَمُ بِطَهَارَتِهَا. حَتَّى يَجُوزُ وَطْؤُهَا بِدُونِ الْغُسْلِ، لَكِنْ لَا يُسْتَحَبُّ. وَلَوْ بَقِيَ مِنْ وَقْتِ فَرْضٍ مِقْدَارُ أَنْ تَقُولَ «اللهُ» يَجِبُ قَضَاؤُهُ، وَإِلَّا فَلَا. فَإِنِ انْقَطَعَ قَبْلَ الْفَجْرِ فِي رَمَضَانَ يُجْزِيهَا صَوْمُهُ وَيَجِبُ قَضَاءُ الْعِشَاءِ، وَإِلَّا فَلَا. فَالْمُعْتَبَرُ الْجُزْءُ الْأَخِيرُ مِنَ الْوَقْتِ، كَمَا فِي الْبُلُوغِ وَالْإِسْلَامِ.

وَإِنِ انْقَطَعَ قَبْلَ أَكْثَرِ الْمُدَّةِ فِيهِمَا، فَهِيَ إِنْ كَانَتْ كِتَابِيَّةً تَطْهُرُ بِمُجَرَّدِ انْقِطَاعِ الدَّمِ، وَإِنْ كَانَتْ مُسْلِمَةً فَزَمَانُ الْغُسْلِ أَوِ التَّيَمُّمِ حَيْضٌ وَنِفَاسٌ. حَتَّى إِذَا لَمْ يَبْقَ بَعْدَهُ مِنَ الْوَقْتِ مِقْدَارُ التَّحْرِيمَةِ

لَا يَجِبُ الْقَضَاءُ، وَلَا يُجْزِيهَا الصَّوْمُ إِنْ لَمْ يَسَعْهُمَا الْبَاقِي مِنَ اللَّيْلِ قَبْلَ الْفَجْرِ.

وَلَا يَجُوزُ وَطْؤُهَا إِلَّا أَنْ تَغْتَسِلَ، أَوْ تَتَيَمَّمَ فَتُصَلِّيَ، أَوْ تَصِيرَ صَلَاةٌ دَيْناً فِي ذِمَّتِهَا. حَتَّى لَوِ انْقَطَعَ قُبَيْلَ طُلُوعِ الشَّمْسِ لَا يَجُوزُ وَطْؤُهَا حَتَّى يَدْخُلَ وَقْتُ الْعَصْرِ، وَكَذَا لَوِ انْقَطَعَ قُبَيْلَ الْعِشَاءِ حَتَّى يَطْلُعَ الْفَجْرُ، إِنْ لَمْ تَغْتَسِلْ أَوْ تَتَيَمَّمْ فَتُصَلِّيَ، إِلَّا أَنْ يَتِمَّ أَكْثَرُ الْمُدَّةِ قَبْلَهُمَا. هَذَا فِي الْمُبْتَدَأَةِ وَالْمُعْتَادَةِ إِذَا انْقَطَعَ فِي عَادَتِهَا أَوْ بَعْدَهَا.

وَأَمَّا إِذَا انْقَطَعَ قَبْلَهَا فَهِيَ فِي حَقِّ الصَّلَاةِ وَالصَّوْمِ كَذَلِكَ. وَأَمَّا الْوَطْءُ فَلَا يَجُوزُ حَتَّى تَمْضِيَ عَادَتُهَا. حَتَّى لَوْ كَانَ حَيْضُهَا عَشَرَةً فَحَاضَتْ ثَلَاثَةً وَطَهَرَتْ سِتَّةً لَا يَحِلُّ وَطْؤُهَا، وَكَذَا النِّفَاسُ.

ثُمَّ إِنَّ الْمَرْأَةَ كُلَّمَا انْقَطَعَ دَمُهَا فِي الْحَيْضِ قَبْلَ ثَلَاثَةِ أَيَّامٍ تَنْتَظِرُ إِلَى آخِرِ الْوَقْتِ الْمُسْتَحَبِّ وُجُوباً، فَإِنْ لَمْ يَعُدْ تَوَضَّأُ فَتُصَلِّي وَتَصُومُ أَوْ تَتَشَبَّهُ. وَإِنْ عَادَ بَطَلَ الْحُكْمُ بِطَهَارَتِهَا فَتَقْعُدُ. وَبَعْدَ الثَّلَاثَةِ إِنِ انْقَطَعَ قَبْلَ الْعَادَةِ فَكَذَلِكَ، لَكِنْ تُصَلِّي بِالْغُسْلِ كُلَّمَا انْقَطَعَ. وَبَعْدَ الْعَادَةِ كَذَلِكَ، لَكِنَّ التَّأْخِيرَ مُسْتَحَبٌّ لَا وَاجِبٌ. وَالنِّفَاسُ كَالْحَيْضِ غَيْرَ أَنَّهُ يَجِبُ الْغُسْلُ فِيهِ كُلَّمَا انْقَطَعَ عَلَى كُلِّ حَالٍ.

الْفَصْلُ الرَّابِعُ: فِي الِاسْتِمْرَارِ.

هُوَ إِنْ وَقَعَ فِي الْمُعْتَادَةِ فَطُهْرُهَا وَحَيْضُهَا مَا اعْتَادَتْ فِي جَمِيعِ الْأَحْكَامِ إِنْ كَانَ طُهْرُهَا أَقَلَّ مِنْ سِتَّةِ أَشْهُرٍ، وَإِلَّا فَيُرَدُّ إِلَى سِتَّةِ أَشْهُرٍ إِلَّا سَاعَةً، وَحَيْضُهَا بِحَالِهِ.

وَإِنْ وَقَعَ فِي الْمُبْتَدَأَةِ فَحَيْضُهَا مِنْ أَوَّلِ الِاسْتِمْرَارِ عَشَرَةٌ وَطُهْرُهَا عِشْرُونَ، ثُمَّ ذَلِكَ دَأْبُهَا. وَنِفَاسُهَا أَرْبَعُونَ، ثُمَّ عِشْرُونَ طُهْرُهَا–إِذْ لَا يَتَوَالَى نِفَاسٌ وَحَيْضٌ – ثُمَّ عَشَرَةٌ حَيْضُهَا، ثُمَّ ذَلِكَ دَأْبُهَا.

وَإِنْ رَأَتْ مُبْتَدَأَةً دَماً وَطُهْراً صَحِيحَيْنِ ثُمَّ اسْتَمَرَّ الدَّمُ تَكُونُ مُعْتَادَةً، وَقَدْ سَبَقَ حُكْمُهَا ؛ لِأَنَّ الْعَادَةَ تَثْبُتُ بِمَرَّةٍ وَاحِدَةٍ لِمَا ذَكَرْنَا فِي الْمُقَدِّمَةِ.

مِثَالُهُ: مُرَاهِقَةٌ رَأَتْ خَمْسَةً دَماً وَأَرْبَعِينَ طُهْراً، ثُمَّ اسْتَمَرَّ الدَّمُ. فَخَمْسَةٌ مِنْ أَوَّلِ الِاسْتِمْرَارِ حَيْضٌ، لَا تُصَلِّي وَلَا تَصُومُ وَلَا تُوطَأُ، وَكَذَا سَائِرُ أَحْكَامِ الْحَيْضِ، ثُمَّ أَرْبَعُونَ طُهْرُهَا تَفْعَلُ هَذِهِ الثَّلَاثَةَ وَغَيْرَهَا مِنْ أَحْكَامِ الطَّاهِرَاتِ.

وَإِنْ رَأَتْ دَماً وَطُهْراً فَاسِدَيْنِ فَلَا اعْتِبَارَ بِهِمَا:

– فَإِنْ كَانَ الطُّهْرُ نَاقِصاً تَكُونُ كَالْمُسْتَمِرِّ دَمُهَا ابْتِدَاءً، عَشَرَةً مِنَ ابْتِدَاءِ الِاسْتِمْرَارِ –وَلَوْ

حُكْماً- حَيْضُهَا، وَعِشْرُونَ طُهْرُهَا، ثُمَّ ذَلِكَ دَأْبُهَا.

مِثَالُهُ: مُرَاهِقَةٌ رَأَتْ أَحَدَ عَشَرَ دَماً وَأَرْبَعَةَ عَشَرَ طُهْراً، ثُمَّ اسْتَمَرَّ الدَّمُ. فَالاسْتِمْرَارُ حُكْماً مِنْ أَوَّلِ مَا رَأَتْ دماً لِمَا عَرَفْتَ أَنَّ الطُّهْرَ النَّاقِصَ كَالدَّمِ الْمُتَوَالِي.

- وَإِنْ كَانَ الطُّهْرُ تَامّاً فَإِنْ لَمْ يَزِدْ عَلَى ثَلاثِينَ فَكَالسَّابِقِ، بِأَنْ رَأَتْ مَثَلاً أَحَدَ عَشَرَ دَماً وَخَمْسَةَ عَشَرَ طُهْراً، ثُمَّ اسْتَمَرَّ الدَّمُ. عَشَرَةٌ مِنْ أَوَّلِ مَا رَأَتْ حَيْضٌ، وَعِشْرُونَ طُهْرٌ، ثُمَّ ذَلِكَ دَأْبُهَا.

وَإِنْ زَادَ، بِأَنْ رَأَتْ مَثَلاً أَحَدَ عَشَرَ دَماً وَعِشْرِينَ طُهْراً، ثُمَّ اسْتَمَرَّ. فَعَشْرَةٌ مِنْ أَوَّلِ مَا رَأَتْ حَيْضٌ، ثُمَّ طُهْرٌ إِلَى أَوَّلِ الاسْتِمْرَارِ، ثُمَّ تَسْتَأْنِفُ مِنْ أَوَّلِ الاسْتِمْرَارِ عَشَرَةٌ حَيْضٌ وَعِشْرُونَ طُهْرٌ، ثُمَّ ذَلِكَ دَأْبُهَا؛ لأَنَّ الطُّهْرَ وَإِنْ كَانَ تَامّاً، أَوَّلُهُ دَمٌ تُصَلِّي بِهِ فَيَفْسُدُ، فَلا يَصْلُحُ لِنَصْبِ الْعَادَةِ.

وَإِنْ كَانَ الدَّمُ صَحِيحاً وَالطُّهْرُ فَاسِداً يُعْتَبَرُ الدَّمُ لا الطُّهْرُ. بِأَنْ رَأَتْ مَثَلاً ثَلاثَةً دَماً، وَخَمْسَةَ عَشَرَ طُهْراً، وَيَوْماً دَماً، وَخَمْسَةَ عَشَرَةَ طُهْراً، ثُمَّ اسْتَمَرَّ الدَّمُ. الثَّلاثَةُ الأُولَى حَيْضٌ، وَالْبَاقِي طُهْرٌ إِلَى الاسْتِمْرَارِ، ثُمَّ تَسْتَأْنِفُ، فَثَلاثَةٌ مِنَ أَوَّلِ الاسْتِمْرَارِ حَيْضٌ وَسَبْعَةٌ وَعِشْرُونَ طُهْرٌ، وَذَلِكَ دَأْبُهَا. وَلَوْ كَانَ الطُّهْرُ الثَّانِي أَرْبَعَةَ عَشَرَ فَطُهْرُهَا خَمْسَةَ عَشَرَ، وَحَيْضُهَا الثَّانِي يَبْتَدِئُ مِنَ الدَّمِ الْمُتَوَسِّطِ إِلَى ثَلاثَةٍ، ثُمَّ طُهْرُهَا خَمْسَةَ عَشَرَ، وَذَلِكَ دَأْبُهَا. إِذْ حِينَئِذٍ يَكُونُ الدَّمُ وَالطُّهْرُ الأَوَّلُ صَحِيحَيْنِ فَيَصْلُحَانِ لِنَصْبِ الْعَادَةِ.

وَإِنْ رَأَتْ طُهْراً صَحِيحاً ثُمَّ اسْتَمَرَّ الدَّمُ، وَلَمْ تَرَ قَبْلَ الطُّهْرِ حَيْضاً أَصْلاً - كَمُرَاهِقَةٍ بَلَغَتْ بِالْحَبَلِ، فَوَلَدَتْ وَرَأَتْ أَرْبَعِينَ دَماً، ثُمَّ خَمْسَةَ عَشَرَ طُهْراً، ثُمَّ اسْتَمَرَّ الدَّمُ - فَحَيْضُهَا عَشَرَةٌ مِنْ أَوَّلِ الاسْتِمْرَارِ، وَطُهْرُهَا خَمْسَةَ عَشَرَ وَذَلِكَ دَأْبُهَا. وَكَذَلِكَ الْحُكْمُ إِذَا زَادَ الطُّهْرُ ؛ لأَنَّهُ صَحِيحٌ يَصْلُحُ لِنَصْبِ الْعَادَةِ.

بِخِلافِ مَا إِذَا زَادَ دَمُهَا عَلَى أَرْبَعِينَ فِي النِّفَاسِ، ثُمَّ رَأَتْ طُهْراً خَمْسَةَ عَشَرَ أَوْ أَكْثَرَ، ثُمَّ اسْتَمَرَّ الدَّمُ، حَيْثُ يَفْسُدُ الطُّهْرُ فَلا يَصلُحُ لِنَصْبِ الْعَادَةِ. فَإِنْ كَانَ بَيْنَ النِّفَاسِ وَالاسْتِمْرَارِ عِشْرُونَ أَوْ أَكْثَرُ فَعَشَرَةٌ مِنْ أَوَّلِ الاسْتِمْرَارِ حَيْضٌ وَعِشْرُونَ طُهْرٌ، وَذَلِكَ دَأْبُهَا، وَإِلَّا أُتِمَّ عِشْرُونَ مِنْ أَوَّلِ الاسْتِمْرَارِ لِلطُّهْرِ، ثُمَّ يُسْتَأْنَفُ عَشَرَةُ حَيْضٍ وَعِشْرُونَ طُهْراً، وَذَلِكَ دَأْبُهَا.

تَنْبِيهٌ: الدِّمَاءُ الْفَاسِدَةُ الْمُسَمَّاةُ بِالاسْتِحَاضَةِ سَبْعَةٌ:

الأَوَّلُ: مَا تَرَاهُ الصَّغِيرَةُ، أَعْنِي: مَنْ لَمْ يَتِمَّ لَهُ تِسْعُ سِنِينَ.

وَالثَّانِي: مَا تَرَاهُ الآيِسَةُ غَيْرَ الأَسْوَدِ وَالأَحْمَرِ.

وَالثَّالِثُ: مَا تَرَاهُ الْحَامِلُ بِغَيْرِ وِلَادَةٍ.

وَالرَّابِعُ: مَا جَاوَزَ أَكْثَرَ الْحَيْضِ وَالنَّفَاسِ إِلَى الْحَيْضِ الثَّانِي.

وَالْخَامِسُ: مَا نَقَصَ مِنَ الثَّلَاثَةِ فِي مُدَّةِ الْحَيْضِ.

وَالسَّادِسُ: مَا عَدَا الْعَادَةَ إِلَى حَيْضٍ غَيْرِهَا، بِشَرْطِ مُجَاوَزَةِ الْعَشْرَةِ وَوُقُوعِ النِّصَابِ فِيهَا.

وَالسَّابِعُ: مَا بَعْدَ مِقْدَارِ عَدَدِ الْعَادَةِ كَذَلِكَ، بِشَرْطِ مُجَاوَزَةِ الْعَشْرَةِ وَعَدَمِ وُقُوعِ النِّصَابِ فِيهَا.

الْفَصْلُ الْخَامِسُ: فِي الْمُضِلَّةِ.

اعْلَمْ أَنَّهُ يَجِبُ عَلَى كُلِّ امْرَأَةٍ حِفْظُ عَادَتِهَا فِي الْحَيْضِ وَالنَّفَاسِ وَالطُّهْرِ عَدَداً وَمَكَاناً. فَإِنْ جُنَّتْ أَوْ أُغْمِيَ عَلَيْهَا أَوْ لَمْ تَهْتَمَّ لِدِينِهَا فِسْقاً، فَنَسِيَتْ عَادَتَهَا فَاسْتَمَرَّ بِهَا الدَّمُ فَعَلَيْهَا أَنْ تَتَحَرَّى. فَإِنِ اسْتَقَرَّ ظَنُّهَا عَلَى مَوْضِعِ حَيْضِهَا وَعَدَدِه عَمِلَتْ بِه، وَإِلَّا فَعَلَيْهَا الأَخْذُ بِالأَحْوَطِ فِي الأَحْكَامِ.

وَلَا يُقَدَّرُ طُهْرُهَا وَحَيْضُهَا إِلَّا فِي حَقِّ الْعِدَّةِ فِي الطَّلَاقِ. يُقَدَّرُ حَيْضُهَا بِعَشْرَةٍ وَطُهْرُهَا بِسِتَّةِ أَشْهُرٍ إِلَّا سَاعَةً ؛ فَتَنْقَضِي عِدَّتُهَا بِتِسْعَةَ عَشَرَ شَهْراً وَعَشَرَةِ أَيَّامٍ غَيْرَ أَرْبَعِ سَاعَاتٍ.

وَلَا تَدْخُلُ الْمَسْجِدَ. وَلَا تَطُوفُ إِلَّا لِلزِّيَارَةِ ثُمَّ تُعِيدُ بَعْدَ عَشَرَةِ أَيَّامٍ، وَلِلصَّدَرِ وَلَا تُعِيدُ. وَلَا تَمَسُّ الْمُصْحَفَ. وَلَا يَجُوزُ وَطْؤُهَا أَبَداً. وَلَا تُصَلِّي وَلَا تَصُومُ تَطَوُّعاً. وَلَا تَقْرَأُ الْقُرْآنَ فِي غَيْرِ الصَّلَاةِ. وَتُصَلِّي الْفَرْضَ وَالْوَاجِبَ وَالسُّنَنَ الْمَشْهُورَةَ. وَتَقْرَأُ فِي كُلِّ رَكْعَةٍ الْفَاتِحَةَ، وَسُورَةً قَصِيرَةً سِوَى مَا عَدَا الأُولَيَيْنِ مِنَ الْفَرْضِ. وَتَقْرَأُ الْقُنُوتَ وَسَائِرَ الدَّعَوَاتِ.

وَكُلَّمَا تَرَدَّدَتْ بَيْنَ الطُّهْرِ وَدُخُولِ الْحَيْضِ صَلَّتْ بِالْوُضُوءِ لِوَقْتِ كُلِّ صَلَاةٍ، وَإِنْ بَيْنَ الطُّهْرِ وَالْخُرُوجِ فَبِالْغُسْلِ كَذَلِكَ، ثُمَّ تُعِيدُ فِي وَقْتِ الثَّانِيَةِ بَعْدَ الْغُسْلِ قَبْلَ الْوَقْتِيَّةِ، وَهَكَذَا تَصْنَعُ فِي كُلِّ صَلَاةٍ. وَإِنْ سَمِعَتْ سَجْدَةً فَسَجَدَتْ لِلْحَالِ سَقَطَتْ عَنْهَا، وَإِلَّا أَعَادَتْهَا بَعْدَ عَشَرَةِ أَيَّامٍ. وَإِنْ كَانَتْ عَلَيْهَا فَائِتَةٌ فَقَضَتْهَا فَعَلَيْهَا إِعَادَتُهَا بَعْدَ عَشَرَةِ أَيَّامٍ قَبْلَ أَنْ تَزِيدَ عَلَى خَمْسَةَ عَشَرَ. وَلَا تُفْطِرُ فِي رَمَضَانَ أَصْلاً.

ثُمَّ إِنْ لَمْ تَعْلَمْ أَنَّ دَوْرَهَا فِي كُلِّ شَهْرٍ مَرَّةً وَأَنَّ ابْتِدَاءَ حَيْضِهَا بِاللَّيْلِ أَوِ النَّهَارِ، أَوْ عَلِمَتْ أَنَّهُ

بِالنَّهارِ، وَكَانَ شَهْرُ رَمَضَانَ ثَلاثِينَ يَجِبُ عَلَيْهَا قَضَاءُ اثْنَيْنِ وَثَلاثِينَ يَوْماً إِنْ قَضَتْ مَوْصُولاً بِرَمَضَانَ، وَإِنْ مَفْصُولاً فَثَمَانِيَةً وَثَلاثِينَ يَوْماً. وَإِنْ كَانَ شَهْرُ رَمَضَانَ تِسْعَةً وَعِشْرِينَ تَقْضِي فِي الْوَصْلِ اثْنَيْنِ وَثَلاثِينَ، وَفِي الْفَصْلِ سَبْعَةً وَثَلاثِينَ.

وَإِنْ عَلِمَتْ أَنَّ ابْتِدَاءَ حَيْضِهَا بِاللَّيْلِ، وَشَهْرُ رَمَضَانَ ثَلاثُونَ فَتَقْضِي فِي الْوَصْلِ وَالْفَصْلِ خَمْسَةً وَعِشْرِينَ. وَإِنْ كَانَ تِسْعَةً وَعِشْرِينَ تَقْضِي فِي الْوَصْلِ عِشْرِينَ، وَفِي الْفَصْلِ أَرْبَعَةً وَعِشْرِينَ.

وَإِنْ عَلِمَتْ أَنَّ حَيْضَهَا فِي كُلِّ شَهْرٍ مَرَّةً وَعَلِمَتْ أَنَّ ابْتِدَاءَهُ بِالنَّهَارِ أَوْ لَمْ تَعْلَمْ أَنَّهُ بِالنَّهَارِ، تَقْضِي اثْنَيْنِ وَعِشْرِينَ يَوْماً مُطْلَقاً. وَإِنْ عَلِمَتْ أَنَّ ابْتِدَاءَهُ بِاللَّيْلِ تَقْضِي عِشْرِينَ مُطْلَقاً.

وَإِنْ عَلِمَتْ أَنَّ حَيْضَهَا فِي كُلِّ شَهْرٍ تِسْعَةً وَعَلِمَتْ أَنَّ ابْتِدَاءَهُ بِاللَّيْلِ، تَقْضِي ثَمَانِيَةَ عَشَرَ مُطْلَقاً. وَإِنْ لَمْ تَعْلَمْ ابْتِدَاءَهُ أَوْ عَلِمَتْ أَنَّهُ بِالنَّهَارِ، تَقْضِي عِشْرِينَ مُطْلَقاً.

وَإِنْ عَلِمَتْ أَنَّ حَيْضَهَا ثَلاثَةٌ، وَنَسِيَتْ طُهْرَهَا يُحْمَلُ عَلَى الأَقَلِّ: خَمْسَةَ عَشَرَ. ثُمَّ إِنْ كَانَ رَمَضَانُ تَامّاً وَعَلِمَتْ أَنَّ ابْتِدَاءَ حَيْضِهَا بِاللَّيْلِ تَقْضِي تِسْعَةً مُطْلَقاً. وَإِنْ لَمْ تَعْلَمْ ابْتِدَاءَهُ أَوْ عَلِمَتْ أَنَّهُ بِالنَّهَارِ تَقْضِي اثْنَي عَشَرَ مُطْلَقاً. وَخَرِّجْ عَلَى مَا ذَكَرْنَا إِنْ كَانَ نَاقِصاً.

وَإِنْ وَجَبَ عَلَيْهَا صَوْمُ شَهْرَيْنِ فِي كَفَّارَةِ الْقَتْلِ أَوْ الإِفْطَارِ قَبْلَ الابْتِلاءِ - إِذِ الإِفْطَارُ فِي هَذَا الابْتِلاءِ لا يُوجِبُ كَفَّارَةً لِتَمَكُّنِ الشُّبْهَةِ - فَإِنْ عَلِمَتْ أَنَّ ابْتِدَاءَ حَيْضِهَا بِاللَّيْلِ وَدَوْرَهَا فِي كُلِّ شَهْرٍ تَصُومُ تِسْعِينَ يَوْماً. وَإِنْ لَمْ تَعْلَمِ الأَوَّلَ تَصُومُ مِائَةً وَأَرْبَعَةً. وَإِنْ لَمْ تَعْلَمِ الثَّانِيَ تَصُومُ مِائَةً. وَإِنْ لَمْ تَعْلَمْهُمَا تَصُومُ مِائَةً وَخَمْسَةَ عَشَرَ.

وَإِنْ وَجَبَ عَلَيْهَا صَوْمُ ثَلاثَةِ أَيَّامٍ فِي كَفَّارَةِ يَمِينٍ وَعَلِمَتْ أَنَّ ابْتِدَاءَ حَيْضِهَا بِاللَّيْلِ تَصُومُ خَمْسَةَ عَشَرَ يَوْماً، أَوْ تَصُومُ ثَلاثَةَ أَيَّامٍ ثُمَّ تُفْطِرُ عَشَرَةً ثُمَّ تَصُومُ ثَلاثَةً. وَإِنْ لَمْ تَعْلَمْ تَصُومُ سِتَّةَ عَشَرَ، أَوْ تَصُومُ ثَلاثَةً وَتُفْطِرُ تِسْعَةً وَتَصُومُ أَرْبَعَةً، أَوْ عَلَى قَلْبِهِ.

وَإِنْ وَجَبَ عَلَيْهَا قَضَاءُ عَشَرَةٍ مِنْ رَمَضَانَ تَصُومُ ضِعْفَهَا، إِمَّا مُتَتَابِعاً، أَوْ تَصُومُ عَشَرَةً فِي عَشَرَةٍ مِنْ شَهْرٍ مَثَلاً، ثُمَّ تَصُومُ مِثْلَهُ فِي عَشْرٍ أُخَرَ مِنْ شَهْرٍ آخَرَ. وَهَذَا الأَخِيرُ يَجْرِي فِيمَا دُونَ الْعَشَرَةِ أَيْضاً.

وَإِنْ طُلِّقَتْ رَجْعِياً يُحْكَمُ بِانْقِطَاعِ الرَّجْعَةِ بِمُضِيِّ تِسْعَةٍ وَثَلاثِينَ. وَهَذَا حُكْمُ الإِضْلالِ الْعَامِّ

وَمَا يَقْرُبُهُ.

وَأَمَّا الخَاصُّ فَمَوْقُوفٌ عَلَى مُقَدِّمَةٍ: وَهِيَ إِنْ أَضَلَّتِ امْرَأَةٌ أَيَّامَهَا فِي ضِعْفِهَا أَوْ أَكْثَرَ، فَلا تَيْقَنُ فِي يَوْمٍ مِنْهَا بِحَيْضٍ، بِخِلافِ مَا إِذَا أَضَلَّتْ فِي أَقَلَّ مِنَ الضِّعْفِ. مَثَلاً: إِذَا أَضَلَّتْ ثَلاثَةً فِي خَمْسَةٍ فَإِنَّهَا تَيْقَنُ بِالحَيْضِ فِي الْيَوْمِ الثَّالِثِ.

فَنَقُولُ إِنْ عَلِمَتْ أَنَّ أَيَّامَهَا ثَلاثَةٌ فَأَضَلَّتْهَا فِي الْعَشَرَةِ الأَخِيرَةِ مِنَ الشَّهْرِ، تُصَلِّي مِنْ أَوَّلِ الْعَشَرَةِ بِالْوُضُوءِ لِوَقْتِ كُلِّ صَلاةٍ ثَلاثَةَ أَيَّامٍ، ثُمَّ تُصَلِّي بَعْدَهَا إِلَى آخِرِ الشَّهْرِ بِالاغْتِسَالِ لِوَقْتِ كُلِّ صَلاةٍ، إِلَّا إِذَا تَذَكَّرَتْ وَقْتَ خُرُوجِهَا مِنَ الْحَيْضِ فَتَغْتَسِلُ فِي كُلِّ يَوْمٍ فِي ذَلِكَ الْوَقْتِ مَرَّةً.

وَإِنْ أَرْبَعَةً فِي عَشَرَةٍ، تُصَلِّي أَرْبَعَةً مِنْ أَوَّلِ الْعَشَرَةِ بِالْوُضُوءِ، ثُمَّ بِالاغْتِسَالِ إِلَى آخِرِ الْعَشْرَةِ. وَقِسْ عَلَيْهِ الْخَمْسَةَ. وَإِنْ سِتَّةً فِي عَشَرَةٍ، تَتَيَقَّنُ بِالْحَيْضِ فِي الْخَامِسِ وَالسَّادِسِ، وَتَفْعَلُ فِي الْبَاقِي مِثْلَ مَا سَبَقَ. وَإِنْ سَبْعَةً فِيهَا، تَتَيَقَّنُ فِي أَرْبَعَةٍ بَعْدَ الثَّلاثَةِ الأُوَلِ بِالْحَيْضِ. وَفِي الثَّمَانِيَةِ، تَتَيَقَّنُ بِالْحَيْضِ فِي سِتَّةٍ بَعْدَ الأَوَّلَيْنِ. وَفِي التِّسْعَةِ، بِثَمَانِيَةٍ بَعْدَ الأَوَّلِ.

وَإِنْ عَلِمَتْ أَنَّهَا تَطْهُرُ فِي آخِرِ الشَّهْرِ فَإِلَى الْعِشْرِينَ فِي طُهْرٍ بِيَقِينٍ، ثُمَّ فِي سَبْعَةٍ بَعْدَ الْعِشْرِينَ تُصَلِّي بِالْوُضُوءِ لِلشَّكِّ فِي الدُّخُولِ، وَتَتْرُكُ الصَّلاةَ فِي الثَّلاثَةِ الأَخِيرَةِ لِلتَّيَقُّنِ بِالْحَيْضِ، ثُمَّ تَغْتَسِلُ فِي آخِرِ الشَّهْرِ.

وَإِنْ عَلِمَتْ أَنَّهَا تَرَى الدَّمَ إِذَا جَاوَزَ الْعِشْرِينَ - وَلا تَدْرِي كَمْ كَانَتْ - تَدَعُ الصَّلاةَ ثَلاثَةً بَعْدَ الْعِشْرِينَ، ثُمَّ تُصَلِّي بِالْغُسْلِ إِلَى آخِرِ الشَّهْرِ. وَعَلَى هَذَا يُخَرَّجُ سَائِرُ الْمَسَائِلِ.

وَإِنْ أَضَلَّتْ عَادَتَهَا فِي النِّفَاسِ، فَإِنْ لَمْ يُجَاوِزِ الدَّمُ أَرْبَعِينَ فَظَاهِرٌ. فَإِنْ جَاوَزَ تَحَرَّى، فَإِنْ لَمْ يَغْلِبْ ظَنُّهَا عَلَى شَيْءٍ قَضَتْ صَلاةَ الأَرْبَعِينَ. فَإِنْ قَضَتْهَا فِي حَالِ اسْتِمْرَارِ الدَّمِ تُعِيدُ بَعْدَ عَشَرَةِ أَيَّامٍ.

وَإِنْ أَسْقَطَتْ سِقْطاً وَلَمْ تَدْرِ أَنَّهُ مُسْتَبِينُ الْخَلْقِ أَوْ لا؛ بِأَنْ أَسْقَطَتْ فِي الْمَخْرَجِ مَثَلاً، وَكَانَ حَيْضُهَا عَشَرَةً وَطُهْرُهَا عِشْرِينَ، وَنِفَاسُهَا أَرْبَعِينَ، وَقَدْ أَسْقَطَتْ مِنْ أَوَّلِ أَيَّامِ حَيْضِهَا تَتْرُكُ الصَّلاةَ عَشَرَةً، ثُمَّ تَغْتَسِلُ وَتُصَلِّي عِشْرِينَ بِالشَّكِّ، ثُمَّ تَتْرُكُ الصَّلاةَ عَشَرَةً، ثُمَّ تَغْتَسِلُ وَتُصَلِّي عِشْرِينَ بِيَقِينٍ. ثُمَّ بَعْدَ ذَلِكَ دَأْبُهَا: حَيْضُهَا عَشَرَةٌ وَطُهْرُهَا عِشْرُونَ إِنِ اسْتَمَرَّ الدَّمُ.

وَلَوْ أَسْقَطَتْ بَعْدَ مَا رَأَتِ الدَّمَ فِي مَوْضِعِ حَيْضِهَا عَشَرَةً وَلَمْ تَدْرِ أَنَّ السِّقْطَ مُسْتَبِينُ الْخَلْقِ أَوْ

لا ، تُصَلِّي مِنْ أَوَّلِ مَا رَأَتْ عَشَرَةً بِالْوُضُوءِ بِالشَّكِّ، ثُمَّ تَغْتَسِلُ، ثُمَّ تُصَلِّي بَعْدَ السِّقْطِ عِشْرِينَ يَوْماً بِالْوُضُوءِ بِالشَّكِّ، ثُمَّ تَتْرُكُ الصَّلاةَ عَشَرَةً بِيَقِينٍ، ثُمَّ تَغْتَسِلُ وَتُصَلِّي عَشَرَةً بِالْوُضُوءِ بِالشَّكِّ، ثُمَّ تَغْتَسِلُ، ثُمَّ تُصَلِّي عَشَرَةً بِالْوُضُوءِ بِيَقِينٍ، ثُمَّ تُصَلِّي عَشَرَةً بِالشَّكِّ.

الْفَصْلُ السَّادِسُ: فِي أَحْكَامِ الدِّمَاءِ الْمَذْكُورَةِ.

أَمَّا أَحْكَامُ الْحَيْضِ فَاثْنَا عَشَرَ، ثَمَانِيَةٌ يَشْتَرِكُ فِيهَا النِّفَاسُ.

الأَوَّلُ: حُرْمَةُ الصَّلاةِ وَالسَّجْدَةِ مُطْلَقاً، وَعَدَمُ وُجُوبِ الْوَاجِبِ مِنْهَا أَدَاءً وَقَضَاءً. لَكِنْ يُسْتَحَبُّ لَهَا إِذَا دَخَلَ وَقْتُ الصَّلاةِ أَنْ تَتَوَضَّأَ، وَتَجْلِسَ عِنْدَ مَسْجِدِ بَيْتِهَا مِقْدَارَ مَا يُمْكِنُ أَدَاءُ الصَّلاةِ فِيهِ تُسَبِّحُ وَتَحْمَدُ ؛ لِئَلا تَزُولَ عَنْهَا عَادَةُ الْعِبَادَةِ.

وَالْمُعْتَبَرُ فِي كُلِّ وَقْتٍ آخِرُهُ مِقْدَارَ التَّحْرِيمَةِ، أَعْنِي: قَوْلَهَا «الله». فَإِنْ حَاضَتْ فِيهِ سَقَطَ عَنْهَا الصَّلاةُ، وَكَذَا إِذَا انْقَطَعَ فِيهِ يَجِبُ قَضَاؤُهَا، وَقَدْ سَبَقَ فِي فَصْلِ الانْقِطَاعِ.

وَكَمَا رَأَتِ الدَّمَ تَتْرُكُ الصَّلاةَ، مُبْتَدَأَةً كَانَتْ أَوْ مُعْتَادَةً. وَكَذَا إِذَا جَاوَزَ عَادَتَهَا فِي عَشَرَةٍ، أَوِ ابْتَدَأَ قَبْلَهَا إِلَّا إِذَا كَانَ الْبَاقِي مِنْ أَيَّامِ طُهْرِهَا مَا لَوْ ضُمَّ إِلَى حَيْضِهَا جَاوَزَ الْعَشَرَةَ.

مَثَلاً: امْرَأَةٌ عَادَتُهَا فِي الْحَيْضِ سَبْعَةٌ وَفِي الطُّهْرِ عِشْرُونَ. رَأَتْ بَعْدَ خَمْسَةَ عَشَرَ مِنْ طُهْرِهَا دَماً تُؤْمَرُ بِالصَّلاةِ إِلَى عِشْرِينَ. وَلَوْ رَأَتْ بَعْدَ سَبْعَةَ عَشَرَ تُؤْمَرُ بِتَرْكِهَا.

ثُمَّ إِذَا انْقَطَعَ قَبْلَ الثَّلاثَةِ، أَوْ جَاوَزَ الْعَشَرَةَ فِي الْمُعْتَادَةِ تُؤْمَرُ بِالْقَضَاءِ.

وَإِنْ سَمِعَتْ آيَةَ السَّجْدَةِ لا سَجْدَةَ عَلَيْهَا.

وَالثَّانِي: حُرْمَةُ الصَّوْمِ مُطْلَقاً. لَكِنْ يَجِبُ قَضَاءُ الْوَاجِبِ مِنْهُ. فَإِنْ رَأَتْ سَاعَةً مِنْ نَهَارٍ -وَلَوْ قُبَيْلَ الْغُرُوبِ- فَسَدَ صَوْمُهَا مُطْلَقاً، وَيَجِبُ قَضَاؤُهُ. وَكَذَا لَوْ شَرَعَتْ فِي صَلاةِ التَّطَوُّعِ أَوِ السُّنَّةِ تَقْضِي، وَفِي صَلاةِ الْفَرْضِ لا. وَكَذَا إِذَا أَوْجَبَتْ عَلَى نَفْسِهَا صَلاةً أَوْ صَوْماً فِي يَوْمٍ فَحَاضَتْ فِيهَا يَجِبُ الْقَضَاءُ، وَلَوْ أَوْجَبَتْهَا فِي أَيَّامِ الْحَيْضِ لا يَلْزَمُهَا شَيْءٌ.

وَالثَّالِثُ: حُرْمَةُ قِرَاءَةِ الْقُرْآنِ وَلَوْ دُونَ آيَةٍ إِذَا قَصَدَتِ الْقِرَاءَةَ. فَإِنْ لَمْ تَقْصِدْ (فَفِي الآيَةِ الطَّوِيلَةِ كَذَلِكَ)، وَفِي الْقَصِيرَةِ كَقَوْلِهِ تَعَالَى: ﴿ثُمَّ نَظَرَ﴾، أَوْ مَا دُونَ الآيَةِ كَـ﴿بِسْمِ اللهِ﴾ لِلتَّيَمُّنِ وَ﴿الْحَمْدُ للهِ﴾ لِلشُّكْرِ فَيَجُوزُ. وَالْمُعَلِّمَةُ تُقَطِّعُ بَيْنَ كُلِّ كَلِمَتَيْنِ. وَتُكْرَهُ قِرَاءَةُ التَّوْرَاةِ وَالإِنْجِيلِ

وَالزَّبُورِ. وَغَسْلُ الْفَمِ لَا يُفِيدُ. وَلَا يُكْرَهُ التَّهَجِّي، وَقِرَاءَةُ الْقُنُوتِ وَسَائِرِ الْأَذْكَارِ وَالدَّعَوَاتِ، وَالنَّظَرُ إِلَى الْمُصْحَفِ.

وَالرَّابِعُ: حُرْمَةُ مَسِّ مَا كُتِبَ فِيهِ آيَةٌ تَامَّةٌ وَلَوْ دِرْهَماً أَوْ لَوْحاً، (وَكُتُبُ الشَّرِيعَةِ: كَالتَّفْسِيرِ وَالْحَدِيثِ وَالْفِقْهِ وَبَيَاضِهِ وَجِلْدِهِ الْمُتَّصِلِ بِهِ، وَلَوْ مَسَّهُ بِحَائِلٍ مُنْفَصِلٍ وَلَوْ كُمَّهُ جَازَ.) وَيَجُوزُ مَسُّ مَا فِيهِ ذِكْرٌ وَدُعَاءٌ، وَلَكِنْ لَا يُسْتَحَبُّ. وَلَا تَكْتُبُ الْقُرْآنَ، وَلَا الْكِتَابَ الَّذِي فِي بَعْضِ سُطُورِهِ آيَةٌ مِنَ الْقُرْآنِ، وَإِنْ لَمْ تَقْرَأْ. وَغَسْلُ الْيَدِ لَا يَنْفَعُ.

وَالْخَامِسُ: حُرْمَةُ الدُّخُولِ فِي الْمَسْجِدِ، إِلَّا فِي الضَّرُورَةِ: كَالْخَوْفِ مِنَ السَّبُعِ أَوِ اللَّصِّ أَوِ الْبَرْدِ أَوِ الْعَطَشِ، وَالْأَوْلَى أَنْ تَتَيَمَّمَ ثُمَّ تَدْخُلَ. وَيَجُوزُ أَنْ تَدْخُلَ مُصَلَّى الْعِيدِ وَزِيَارَةَ الْقُبُورِ.

وَالسَّادِسُ: حُرْمَةُ الطَّوَافِ.

وَالسَّابِعُ: حُرْمَةُ الْجِمَاعِ وَاسْتِمْتَاعُ مَا تَحْتَ الْإِزَارِ. وَتَثْبُتُ الْحُرْمَةُ بِإِخْبَارِهَا. وَإِنْ جَامَعَهَا طَائِعَيْنِ أَثِمَا، وَعَلَيْهِمَا التَّوْبَةُ وَالِاسْتِغْفَارُ. وَيُسْتَحَبُّ أَنْ يَتَصَدَّقَ بِدِينَارٍ إِنْ كَانَ فِي أَوَّلِ الْحَيْضِ، وَبِنِصْفِهِ إِنْ كَانَ فِي آخِرِهِ.(وَيُكَفَّرُ مُسْتَحِلُّهُ.)

وَالثَّامِنُ: وُجُوبُ الْغُسْلِ أَوِ التَّيَمُّمِ عِنْدَ الِانْقِطَاعِ.

وَأَمَّا الْأَرْبَعَةُ الْمُخْتَصَّةُ بِالْحَيْضِ:

فَأَوَّلُهَا: تَعَلُّقُ انْقِضَاءِ الْعِدَّةِ بِهِ. وَثَانِيهَا: (الِاسْتِبْرَاءُ.) وَثَالِثُهَا: الْحُكْمُ بِبُلُوغِهَا. وَرَابِعُهَا: الْفَصْلُ بَيْنَ طَلَاقَيِ السُّنَّةِ وَالْبِدْعَةِ.

وَأَمَّا الِاسْتِحَاضَةُ فَحَدَثٌ أَصْغَرُ كَالرُّعَافِ.

تَذْنِيبٌ: فِي حُكْمِ الْجَنَابَةِ وَالْحَدَثِ.

أَمَّا الْأَوَّلُ: فَكَالنِّفَاسِ، إِلَّا أَنَّهُ لَا يُسْقِطُ الصَّلَاةَ، وَلَا يُحَرِّمُ الصَّوْمَ وَالْجِمَاعَ وَلَوْ قَبْلَ الْوُضُوءِ. وَإِذَا أَرَادَ أَنْ يَأْكُلَ أَوْ يَشْرَبَ يَغْسِلُ يَدَيْهِ وَفَمَهُ. وَيَجُوزُ خُرُوجُهُ لِحَوَائِجِهِ.

وَأَمَّا حُكْمُ الْحَدَثِ فَثَلَاثَةٌ:

الْأَوَّلُ: حُرْمَةُ الصَّلَاةِ وَالسَّجْدَةِ مُطْلَقاً.

وَالثَّانِي: حُرْمَةُ مَسِّ مَا فِيهِ آيَةٌ تَامَّةٌ، وَكُتُبِ التَّفْسِيرِ ؛ وَلَوْ بَعْدَ غَسْلِ الْيَدِ. وَلَكِنْ يَجُوزُ دَفْعُ

الْمُصْحَفِ إِلَى الصِّبْيانِ. وَلا بَأْسَ بِمَسِّ كُتُبِ الأَحَادِيثِ وَالْفِقْهِ وَالأَذْكَارِ، وَالْمُسْتَحَبُّ أَنْ لا يَفْعَلَ.

وَالثَّالِثُ: كَرَاهَةُ الطَّوَافِ. وَيَجُوزُ لَهُ قِرَاءَةُ الْقُرْآنِ، وَدُخُولُ الْمَسْجِدِ.

[أَحْكَامُ الْمَعْذُورِ]

ثُمَّ إِنَّ الْحَدَثَ إِنِ اسْتَوْعَبَ وَقْتَ صَلاةٍ ؛ بِأَنْ لَمْ يُوجَدْ فِيهِ زَمَانٌ خَالٍ عَنْهُ يَسَعُ الْوُضُوءَ وَالصَّلاةَ، يُسَمَّى عُذْراً، وَصَاحِبُهُ: مَعْذُوراً، وَصَاحِبَ الْعُذْرِ.

وَحُكْمُهُ: أَنْ لا يَنْتَقِضَ وُضُوؤُهُ مِنْ ذَلِكَ الْحَدَثِ بِتَجَدُّدِهِ، إِلَّا عِنْدَ خُرُوجِ وَقْتِ مَكْتُوبَةٍ. فَيُصَلِّي بِهِ فِي الْوَقْتِ مَا شَاءَ مِنَ الْفَرَائِضِ وَالنَّوَافِلِ. وَلا يَجُوزُ لَهُ أَنْ يَمْسَحَ خُفَّهُ إِلَّا فِي الْوَقْتِ. وَلا تَجُوزُ إِمَامَتُهُ لِغَيْرِ الْمَعْذُورِ.

ثُمَّ فِي الْبَقَاءِ: لا يُشْتَرَطُ الاسْتِيعَابُ، بَلْ يَكْفِي وُجُودُهُ فِي كُلِّ وَقْتٍ مَرَّةً. وَلَوْ لَمْ يُوجَدْ فِي وَقْتٍ تَامٍّ سَقَطَ الْعُذْرُ مِنْ أَوَّلِ الانْقِطَاعِ. حَتَّى لَوِ انْقَطَعَ فِي أَثْنَاءِ الْوُضُوءِ أَوِ الصَّلاةِ وَدَامَ الانْقِطَاعُ إِلَى آخِرِ الْوَقْتِ الثَّانِي يُعِيدُ تِلْكَ الصَّلاةَ. وَإِنْ عَادَ قَبْلَ خُرُوجِ الْوَقْتِ الثَّانِي لا يُعِيدُ.

وَلَوْ عَرَضَ بَعْدَ دُخُولِ وَقْتِ فَرْضٍ انْتَظَرَ إِلَى آخِرِهِ فَإِنْ لَمْ يَنْقَطِعْ يَتَوَضَّأُ وَيُصَلِّي. ثُمَّ إِنِ انْقَطَعَ فِي أَثْنَاءِ الْوَقْتِ الثَّانِي يُعِيدُ تِلْكَ الصَّلاةَ. وَإِنِ اسْتَوْعَبَ الْوَقْتَ الثَّانِيَ لا يُعِيدُ لِثُبُوتِ الْعُذْرِ حِينَئِذٍ مِنَ ابْتِدَاءِ الْعُرُوضِ.

وَإِنَّمَا قُلْنَا: «مِنْ ذَلِكَ الْحَدَثِ» إِذْ لَوْ تَوَضَّأَ مِنْ آخَرَ فَسَالَ مِنْ عُذْرِهِ نُقِضَ وُضُوؤُهُ وَإِنْ لَمْ يَخْرُجِ الْوَقْتُ، وَإِنْ لَمْ يَسِلْ مِنْ عُذْرِهِ لا يَنْتَقِضُ وَإِنْ خَرَجَ الْوَقْتُ.

وَإِنَّمَا قُلْنَا: «بِتَجَدُّدِهِ» إِذْ لَوْ تَوَضَّأَ مِنْ عُذْرِهِ فَعَرَضَ حَدَثٌ آخَرُ يَنْتَقِضُ وُضُوؤُهُ فِي الْحَالِ. وَإِنْ لَمْ يَعْرِضْ وَلَمْ يَسِلْ مِنْ عُذْرِهِ لا يُنْقَضُ بِخُرُوجِ الْوَقْتِ. وَإِنْ سَالَ الدَّمُ مِنْ أَحَدِ مِنْخَرَيْهِ فَقَطْ فَتَوَضَّأَ ثُمَّ سَالَ مِنَ آخَرَ انْتَقَضَ وُضُوؤُهُ. وَإِنْ سَالَ مِنْهُمَا فَتَوَضَّأَ فَانْقَطَعَ مِنْ أَحَدِهِمَا لا يَنْتَقِضُ.

وَالْجُدَرِيُّ وَالدَّمَامِيلُ قُرُوحٌ، لا وَاحِدَةٌ. حَتَّى لَوْ تَوَضَّأَ وَبَعْضُهَا غَيْرُ سَائِلٍ ثُمَّ سَالَ انْتَقَضَ. وَلَوْ تَوَضَّأَ وَكُلُّهَا سَائِلٌ لا يَنْتَقِضُ.

وَلَوْ خَرَجَ الْوَقْتُ وَهُوَ فِي الصَّلاةِ يَسْتَأْنِفُ وَلا يَبْنِي؛ لأَنَّ الانْتِقَاضَ بِالْحَدَثِ السَّابِقِ حَقِيقَةً، إِلَّا أَنْ يَنْقَطِعَ قَبْلَ الْوُضُوءِ وَدَامَ حَتَّى خَرَجَ الْوَقْتُ وَهُوَ فِي الصَّلاةِ فَلا يَنْتَقِضُ وُضُوؤُهُ وَلا تَفْسُدُ

صَلاتُهُ حِينَئِذٍ.

وَلَوْ تَوَضَّأَ المَعْذُورُ بِغَيْرِ حَاجَةٍ ثُمَّ سَالَ عُذْرُهُ انْتَقَضَ وُضُوؤُهُ. وَكَذَا لَوْ تَوَضَّأَ لِصَلاةٍ قَبْلَ وَقْتِها.

وَإِنْ قَدَرَ المَعْذُورُ عَلَى مَنْعِ السَّيَلانِ بِالرَّبْطِ وَنَحْوِهِ يَلْزَمُهُ، وَيَخْرُجُ مِنَ الْعُذْرِ، بِخِلافِ الحَائِضِ كَمَا سَبَقَ.

وَإِنْ سَالَ عِنْدَ السُّجُودِ وَلَمْ يَسِلْ بِدُونِهِ يُومِئُ قَائِماً أَوْ قَاعِداً. وَكَذَا لَوْ سَالَ عِنْدَ الْقِيَامِ يُصَلِّي قَاعِداً، كَمَا أَنَّ مَنْ عَجَزَ عَنِ الْقِرَاءَةِ لَوْ قَامَ يُصَلِّي قَاعِداً، بِخِلافِ مَن لَوْ اسْتَلْقَى لَمْ يَسِلْ فَإِنَّهُ لا يُصَلِّي مُسْتَلْقِياً.

وَمَا أَصَابَ ثَوْبَ المَعْذُورِ أَكْثَرُ مِنْ قَدْرِ الدِّرْهَمِ فَعَلَيْهِ غَسْلُهُ إِنْ كَانَ مُفِيداً. وَإِنْ كَانَ بِحَالٍ لَوْ غَسَلَهُ تَنَجَّسَ ثَانِياً قَبْلَ الْفَرَاغِ مِنَ الصَّلاةِ جَازَ أَنْ لا يَغْسِلَهُ.

Appendix 2: Sample Record Charts

The following charts are ideas of how one can keep record of their menses and lochial. Charts like these could be copied into a small notebook and personal details filled in.

MENSTRUATION

Sample One Year: 2006

Menses/Tuhr	Start	End	Total*
M	1-1 10 am	1-7 12:45 pm	6 days 3 hrs
T	1-7 1:00 pm	2-1 4:45 pm	25 days 4 hrs
M	2-1 5:00 pm	2-8 8:45 pm	7 days 4 hrs

Sample Two Year: 2006

Start	End	Total *	M/T	Comments
10 am *Jan* 1	12:45 am *Jan* 7	6 days 3 hrs	M	normal
1 pm *Jan* 7	4:45 pm *Jan* 31	24 days 4 hrs	T	ovulated Jan 14
5 pm *Jan* 31	8:15 pm *Feb* 7	7 days 3½ hrs	M	Day 1-v painful
8:30 pm *Feb* 7	10 pm *Feb* 28	21 days 1½ hrs	T	ovulated Feb 14

LOCHIA

Sample One

Preg	Start	End	Total*	Name
1st	1-1-04 7 am	2-05-04 10:45 am	35 days 4 hrs	*Ahmad*
2nd	2-01-05 5 pm	2-28-05 9:45pm	27 days 5 hrs	Misc 5 months
3rd	8-1-06 6 am	8-31-06 12:45 pm	30 days 7 hrs	*Khadija*

Sample Two

Name	Start	End	Total*	Pregnancy
Ahmad	7 am *Jan* 1, 04	10:45 am *Feb* 5	35days 4 hrs	1st
Misc. 4 m	5 pm *Feb* 1,05	9:45 pm *Feb* 28	27 days 5 hrs	2nd
Khadija	6 am *Aug* 1, 06	12:45 pm *Aug* 31	30 days 7 hrs	3rd

* Approximately 15 minutes is added for the ghusl when the bleeding is less than the maximum because it is considered part of the menstrual/lochial period.

Sample Menstrual Calendar

Year: 2005

	1	2	3	4	5	6	7	8	9	10	11	12	13	14	15	16	17	18	19	20	21	22	23	24	25	26	27	28	29	30	31	*Times
Jan	✓	✓	✓	✓	✓	✓	✓																									9:30am/7pm
Feb			✓	✓	✓	✓	✓	✓	✓	✓																						10pm/9am
Mar						✓	✓	✓	✓	✓	✓	✓																				11am/8pm
Apr									✓	✓	✓	✓	✓	✓																		6am/11pm
May									✓	✓	✓	✓	✓	✓	✓																	10:30am/9pm
Jun								✓	✓	✓	✓	✓	✓	✓	✓																	11pm/7:30am
Jul										✓	✓	✓	✓	✓	✓	✓																8am/5pm
Aug												✓	✓	✓	✓	✓	✓	✓														9am/3pm
Sep													✓	✓	✓	✓	✓	✓														7am/10pm
Oct															✓	✓	✓	✓	✓	✓	✓	✓										9pm/5am
Nov																		✓	✓	✓	✓	✓	✓	✓								4am/11pm
Dec																						✓	✓	✓	✓	✓	✓	✓				8pm/1pm

* Starting and Ending times should be recorded in the right side column.

** If the bleeding is less than the maximum (10 days/40 days), add the ghusl time, about 15 minutes, to the ending time because it is considered part of the menstrual or lochial period.

Sample Menstrual-Lochial Calendar

Year: 2005

	1	2	3	4	5	6	7	8	9	10	11	12	13	14	15	16	17	18	19	20	21	22	23	24	25	26	27	28	29	30	31	*Times
Jan	✓	✓	✓	✓	✓																											10pm/5am
Feb																											✓					11pm
Mar		✓																														2pm
Apr			✓																													5pm
May																																
Jun																																
Jul																																
Aug																																
Sep																																
Oct														✓	✓	✓	✓	✓	✓	✓	✓	✓	✓	✓	✓	✓	✓	✓	✓	✓	✓	Birth 7:30am
Nov	✓	✓	✓	✓	✓	✓	✓	✓	✓	✓	✓	✓	✓	✓																		4pm
Dec																									✓	✓	✓	✓	✓	✓	✓	10:30am/9pm

* Starting and Ending times should be recorded in the right side column.

** If the bleeding is less than the maximum (10 days/40 days), add the ghusl time, about 15 minutes, to the ending time because it is considered part of the menstrual or lochial period.

Sample - Make Additional Copies For Yourself - Family - Friends - Sample - Make Additional Copies For Yourself - Family - Friends - Sample

✂ -

Yearly Menstrual-Lochial Calendar

Name: Year:

	1	2	3	4	5	6	7	8	9	10	11	12	13	14	15	16	17	18	19	20	21	22	23	24	25	26	27	28	29	30	31	*Times
Jan																																
Feb																																
Mar																																
Apr																																
May																																
Jun																																
Jul																																
Aug																																
Sep																																
Oct																																
Nov																																
Dec																																

* Starting and Ending times should be recorded in the right side column.

** If the bleeding is less than the maximum (10 days/40 days), add the ghusl time, about 15 minutes, to the ending time because it is considered part of the menstrual or lochial period.

Sample - Make Additional Copies For Yourself - Family - Friends - Sample - Make Additional Copies For Yourself - Family - Friends - Sample

Yearly Menstrual-Lochial Calendar

Name: Year:

	1	2	3	4	5	6	7	8	9	10	11	12	13	14	15	16	17	18	19	20	21	22	23	24	25	26	27	28	29	30	31	*Times
Jan																																
Feb																																
Mar																																
Apr																																
May																																
Jun																																
Jul																																
Aug																																
Sep																																
Oct																																
Nov																																
Dec																																

* Starting and Ending times should be recorded in the right side column.

** If the bleeding is less than the maximum (10 days/40 days), add the ghusl time, about 15 minutes, to the ending time because it is considered part of the menstrual or lochial period.

Sample - Make Additional Copies For Yourself - Family - Friends - Sample - Make Additional Copies For Yourself - Family - Friends - Sample

✂ -

Yearly Menstrual-Lochial Calendar

Name: Year:

	1	2	3	4	5	6	7	8	9	10	11	12	13	14	15	16	17	18	19	20	21	22	23	24	25	26	27	28	29	30	31	*Times
Jan																																
Feb																																
Mar																																
Apr																																
May																																
Jun																																
Jul																																
Aug																																
Sep																																
Oct																																
Nov																																
Dec																																

* Starting and Ending times should be recorded in the right side column.

** If the bleeding is less than the maximum (10 days/40 days), add the ghusl time, about 15 minutes, to the ending time because it is considered part of the menstrual or lochial period.

Works Cited

1. 'Abidin, Muhammad Amin ibn 'Umar. *Hashiya Ibn 'Abidin*. 16 vols. Damascus: Dar al-Thaqafah wa al-Turath, 2000–[in progress].

2. ————. *Manhal al-Waridin min Bihar al-Fayd 'ala Dhukhr al-Muta'ahhilin fi Masa'il al-Hayd*. Edited and annotated by Hedaya Hartford and Ashraf Muneeb. Damascus: Dar al-Fikr, 2005.

3. al-Abyani, Muhammad Zaid. *Sharh al-Ahkam al-Shari'yya fi al-Ahwal al-Shakhsiyya*. 3 vols. Photocopy. Damascus, n.d.

4. al-Birgivi, Muhammad Pir 'Ali. *Dhukhr al-Muta'ahhilin wa al-Nisa' fi ta'rif al-Athar wa al-Dima'*. Edited and annotated by Hedaya Hartford and Ashraf Muneeb. Damascus: Dar al-Fikr, 2005.

5. Carlson, Karen J., Stephanie A. Eisenstat, and Terra Ziporyn. *The Harvard Guide to Women's Health*. Cambridge, Mass: Harvard University Press, 1996.

6. Hartford, Hedaya and Ashraf Muneeb, *Irshad al-Mukallafin ila Daqa'iq Dhukhr al-Muta'ahhilin*. Damascus: Dar al-Fikr, 2005.

7. al-Kasani, 'Ala al-Din Abu Bakr ibn Sa'ud, *Bada'i al-Sana'i fi Tartib al-Shara'i*. 6 vols. Beirut: Mu'assasa al-Tarikh al-'Arabi, 1997.

8. *Merck Manual of Medical Information Home Edition*. Whitehouse Station, New Jersey: Merck Research Laboratories, 1997.

9. Northrup, Christiane. *Women's Bodies, Women's Wisdom*. New York: Bantam Books, 1998.

10. al-Shurunbulali, Hasan ibn 'Ammar ibn 'Ali. *Imdad al-Fatah sharh Nur al-Iydah wa Najat al-Arwah*. Damascus, n.d.

11. al-Tahtawi, Ahmad ibn Muhammad ibn Isma'il, *Hashiya al-Tahtawi 'ala Maraqi al-Falah sharh Nur al-'Idah*. Istanbul: Dar al-Ada', n.d.

Imam Birgivi

Imam Birgivi is Muhammad ibn Pir 'Ali ibn Iskandar al-Rumi, Abu Mustafa Muhyi al-Din, Taqi al-Din, or Zain al-Din Birgivi Mehmed Efendi. Although his name has been orthographically rendered as Birgili, Birgli, Birkili, Birgilu, Berkeley, Berkawi, the most accurate spelling is Birgivi, derived from the town Birge in Turkey where he lived the last years of his life.

He was born in southwestern Anatolia in the Bekteshler village of the Kepsut region of the Balikesir Governate, in 929/1523. He lived during the height of the Ottoman Empire under the reigns of Sultan Suleiman the Magnificent A.D. 1520–1566 and his son Sultan Salim II A.D. 1566–1574.

He was raised in a religious scholarly family. His father, Pir 'Ali Efendi, was a famous professor in Balikesir, admired both for his scholarship and virtue. From a very young age Imam al-Birgivi devoted himself to mastering the Islamic sciences. He learned Arabic literature, Hanafi jurisprudence, fundamentals of Islamic law, Qur'anic commentary, Hadith, tenets of faith, logic, and so forth. He memorized the Qur'an, as that was the norm for scholars of his time. He was an authority in the fundamentals of the Islamic sciences and the Arabic language. He studied under his father Pir 'Ali Efendi, 'Ataullah Efendi, Küçük Shams al-Din Efendi, Ahizade Qaramani Mehmed Efendi, Abdurrahman Efendi, and the Chief Military Judge of the Ottoman Empire Kazasker Abdurrahman Qaramani Efendi.

He lived the life of those dedicated to the Hereafter. He had noble character and sought the true knowledge of Allah and the religious sciences. He was a prominent scholar and moralist who combined knowledge and godfearingness, externally and internally, and spent his life teaching and writing.

Deep in understanding and meticulous in detail of the subjects he mastered, he authored eleven works in Islamic jurisprudence, three in Qur'anic commentary, thirteen in tenets of faith, three in Hadith, four in Sufism, ten on the Arabic language, as well as others in logic, etiquette, biography, politics, astronomy, and legal opinion.

His influence is felt to this day. His works of the Arabic language are among the classics in teaching and learning Arabic. His book *al-Tariqa al-Muhammadiyyah* (The Path of Muhammad) is still used in the most important faculties of theology and in universities of many Muslim countries. His manual on menstruation and related issues is the primary reference for the Hanafi school of jurisprudence, and in the words of Imam Ibn 'Abidin, is "a work of genius unmatched, the like of which no eye has seen."

At the age of fifty in 981/1573, he died of the plague on his way to Istanbul. He was taken back to his village, Birge, and buried just northeast of it where his grave remains.